THE MORAL VIRTUES
AND THEOLOGICAL ETHICS

THE MORAL VIRTUES
AND THEOLOGICAL ETHICS

Romanus Cessario, O.P.

UNIVERSITY OF NOTRE DAME PRESS
NOTRE DAME   LONDON

Library of Congress Cataloging-in-Publication Data
Cessario, Romanus.
  The moral virtues and theological ethics / Romanus
Cessario.
      p.   cm.
  Includes bibliographical references and index.
  ISBN 0-268-01388-8 — ISBN 0-268-01389-6 (pbk.)
  1. Virtues. 2. Christian ethics—Catholic authors.   I.
Title.
BV4630.C47   1990
241'.4—dc20   90-70854
                                                  CIP

FOR
MICHAEL PAUL AND MARY GERTRUDE CESSARIO
IN PIAM MEMORIAM

CONTENTS

ACKNOWLEDGMENTS

Preparation for the present volume actually began some ten years ago when circumstances at the Dominican House of Studies in Washington, D.C., obliged me to give some lectures in moral theology. Although theological interest in the moral virtues had not then peaked, the course nonetheless enticed certain students in the Washington Theological Consortium. John Ehmann, Administrative Director of the University of Notre Dame Press, took note of this course and urged the publication of its *scriptum*. First of all, then, I would like to express my appreciation to Mr. Ehmann for this initiative and his subsequent encouragement. At the same time, I gratefully recognize the contributions made by the diverse theological students who, for various reasons, assisted at the lectures in Washington.

Although modern technology has moved us far beyond the collaborative methods of the medieval scriptoria, the production of a book-length manuscript still requires the work of different people. I am grateful, then, to Robert Twele, O.F.M. Conv., and Stephen Dominic Hayes, O.P., for their technical assistances and to John McIntyre, S.J., and Russell Shaw for their literary services. Daniel Bourgeois, Fraternité des Moines Apostoliques, and Peter John Cameron, O.P., also contributed verily and variously to the refinement of the text.

Finally, I owe a debt of gratitude to the Dominican Fathers at the Albertinum, Fribourg (Switzerland). During my first sabbatical year from teaching, the Prior, Guy Bedouelle, O.P., and community welcomed me with characteristic generosity and warmth, so that I was able to complete work on this project promptly, easily, and joyfully. According to established custom, I am especially happy to dedicate this study to my parents, who, during their lifetimes, gave me concrete example of the virtues, both acquired and infused.

David Hall
Phil. of Biological Science
1974.

___

L'enjeu de la Phil. Méd.
André de Muralt
Brill, 1991.

___

Richard Dawkins.
.C. O'Brien   591.5
auth 2 a 2ae, 1-7, vol 31
Dewan objectum. Arch. d'hist.
   Doctrinale etc. 1981, 37-96.   D322
~~Savi~~   2~~ft.4~~ 64-78
               91, 93-94
        ~~C378~~.

Ingham.

The Saint Ignatius Institute is inaugurating the Flocchini Forum for a contemporary consideration of Catholicism and culture. We will endeavor to bring dynamic and expert speakers on a variety of topics which have very much to do with everyday life.

Please join us on both evenings of the Forum, but especially for dinner and the Saturday evening lecture. Part of our reason for the occasion is to gather our academic community, alumni included, to keep the intellectual pot stirred.

I warmly invite all of you for our weekend of seeking truth and good cheer.

In Christ,
John W. Galten

INTRODUCTION

In order to explicate what Christians believe about the moral life, theological ethics has long employed both the vocabulary and the rhetoric of virtue theory. Arguably, one can discover the substance of a well-developed theology of virtue even in the earliest patristic writers. But a fourth-century Christian apologist, Lactantius, gave the subject of virtue in the Christian life its first embellished treatment in his *Divinae Institutiones*.[1] Of course, justification for this practice derives from the New Testament itself. Even a casual perusal of the Gospels and the writings of the apostles reveals the specificity of Christian teaching on the virtues. In general, the New Testament presents virtue as an interior principle of the moral life which directs the individual's relationship with God and with neighbor. As such, Christian virtue remains a stable reality, something which firmly establishes in the believer the capacity to accomplish those deeds which are worthy of the Kingdom of God.

To cite but a single example, consider the parable of the wise and foolish maidens (Mt 25:1–13). Jesus compares those ready to welcome the reign of God with five prudent maidens, whose virtuous character primed them even for the unexpected arrival of the bridegroom. The principal point of the parable illustrates the kind of preparedness Jesus expects of his disciples, but the wise or prudent maidens also represent all those who possess the ensemble of virtues which characterize a complete Christian life. The burning oil lamps which they carry into the wedding feast symbolically portray Christian wisdom, the crown of the other gifts of the Holy Spirit and of the infused moral virtues. This Christian wisdom empowers all those who embrace prudence and the other moral virtues to fulfill the requirements of an integral and holy life. At the same time, the wise maidens present themselves as both qualified and eager to enter into the company of Christ. As a biblical symbol, the marriage feast represents beatitude, the definitive embrace of divine love for the creature, which constitutes the final perfection that Christian belief and practice achieve in each one of us.

The New Testament authors may use the term "virtue" sparingly, but, as in so many similar cases, the substance of the concept pervades their moral teaching. Moreover, ample documentation exists to show that some of the earliest moral instruction in the Church uses the language of virtue. In fact, St. Augustine spoke about the virtue of Christ himself as the principal support of the believer's whole life.[2] This justifies his confidence when, commenting on the verse of the psalm, "My mouth is filled with thy praise, and with thy glory all the day" (Ps 71:8), St. Augustine asks: "What does it mean 'all the day'?" He gives this reply: "It means without interruption: In good times, because Christ consoles us; in bad times, because he corrects us; before we came to be, because Christ made us; as long as we exist, because he has given us salvation; when we sin, because Christ ignores it; when we are converted, because Christ urges it; when we shall have endured, because Christ crowns our perseverance."[3] Clearly, St. Augustine understood the controlling truth of the Christian religion, namely, that our lives find fulfillment only by following the rhythm which Christ himself establishes.

This book provides a general introduction to the study of the Christian moral virtues. It is a practical book, which purports to help the interested reader establish the rhythm of Christ-centered virtue in his or her own life. By and large, Christians are accustomed to examine their conscience by referring to the Decalogue and, for Roman Catholics, to the commandments of the Church. Contemporary debate about the principles of moral theology, the role of an ecclesiastical Magisterium, the prerogatives of personal conscience, and other matters have surely altered the manner in which the believer undertakes this examination of conscience. Even though revisionism interprets rules differently from the procedure endorsed by pre-conciliar casuistry, revisionist moral theology still remains rule-centered.[4] Because neither casuistry nor revisionism figure largely in the present study, this book represents a fresh approach to theological ethics. *The Moral Virtues and Theological Ethics* illustrates a moral life based on the traditional virtues of Christian literature and instruction, such as a St. Augustine would have taught to those under his pastoral care.

Obedience to divine and ecclesiastical precepts holds an important place in the history and practice of moral theology. This book, however, seeks to retrieve an alternative convention. Surely the pastoral directions of the Second Vatican Council (1962–1965) go a long way to explain why such a retrieval remains both necessary and urgent. A theology of moral virtue represents a long-standing tradition in the Christian Church. The schoolmen of the Middle Ages, inspired by patristic texts and aided by classical philosophy, developed different models to explain the dynamics of the moral virtues. But the voluntarist emphases associated with the *via moderna* and the harvest of late medieval theology cut short the development of this paradigm. Because it stresses a narrow view of will power as the principal cause of moral action, a voluntarist perspective favors norms and precepts as the preferred subject matter for ethical discourse. Thus, from the Renaissance until the middle of this century, moral legalism predominated in both Roman Catholic and reformed circles. Few people are accustomed then to think about their moral lives in terms of the cultivation of virtue.

Nevertheless, the tradition enumerates seven primary virtues which comprise the substance of an authentic Christian life: faith, hope, and charity, prudence, justice, fortitude, and temperance. First of all, Christian doctrine considers the theological or divine virtues. Since their exercise relates the believer directly to God, these virtues of faith, hope, and charity occupy a principal place in Christian living. Strictly speaking, no human analogues exist for the theological virtues; only the justifying power of the Holy Spirit causes them to come about in the believer. About these virtues, St. Paul testifies: "For now we see in a mirror dimly, but then face to face. Now I know in part; then I shall understand fully, even as I have been fully understood. So faith, hope, love abide, these three; but the greatest of these is love" (1 Cor 13:12,13). Since the theological virtues comprise a distinct area of theological investigation, they figure only indirectly in the present study.

Many theologians recognize that the theological virtues alone, even with charity, cannot sufficiently inform the believer with what is required to act properly in every situation. This explains why the Christian tradition also incorporates the moral virtues of prudence, justice, fortitude, and temperance. These cardinal virtues, as they are called, provide the focal points for at least fifty other allied and auxiliary virtues. Altogether these moral virtues constitute the substance of a happy life, that is, a life which embodies every quality required for a complete and flourishing human existence. In other terms, the moral virtues embrace as their proper matter all the ordinary and extraordinary affairs which comprise an ethical life.

During the last decade, philosophical work on the moral virtues advanced considerably.[5] But Christian faith necessarily changes the way one considers virtue. This text aims at an evaluation of the moral virtues from the standpoint of Christian belief.[6] Theological ethics simply mean the moral teaching of the New Testament as developed within the interpretive tradition of the Christian Church. At certain moments throughout its history, the Magisterium of the Church has given specific direction to this development. And while dogmatic issues usually draw the most attention from historians of doctrine, the Church has always claimed that her teaching authority extends to matters which pertain to the actual practice of the Christian life as well. "For the Catholic Church is by the will of Christ the teacher of truth. It is her duty to proclaim and teach with authority the truth which is Christ and, at the same time, to declare and confirm by her authority the principles of the moral order which spring from human nature itself."[7]

Of course, it would be impossible to consider in a single volume every virtue which one or another Christian author has treated during the course of nearly two millennia. The interpretive tradition on morals and the moral virtues comprises too vast a field for such an undertaking. Nor does the present volume aspire even to take up explicitly each of the cardinal moral virtues. Josef Pieper's classic *Four Cardinal Virtues* (Notre Dame, 1965) admirably accomplishes that task. Rather, this book presents a general theory of the virtues which holds good for any particular moral virtue; it explains how the virtues work in our everyday lives. And since the inquiry considers the moral virtues principally within the context of the Christian life, this requires that the chapters address certain theological issues. In brief, this book talks about how the moral virtues perform within a life of Christian faith animated by charity, and so fulfills the Council's wish that moral theology "should show the nobility of the Christian vocation of the faithful, and their obligation to bring forth fruit in charity for the life of the world.[8]

Although the theology of the virtues presented in this volume draws upon many resources, the teaching of St. Thomas Aquinas remains a central influence. In the thirteenth century, Aquinas distinguished himself by developing a moral theology of the virtues.[9] The *secunda pars,* which contains his treatise on the virtues and theological ehtics, makes up the largest section of his three-part *Summa theologiae.* Moreover, on the basis of a large sampling of texts, the *secunda secundae,* a synopsis of vices and virtues, accounts for a higher percentage of extant manuscripts than any other single section of Aquinas's celebrated textbook for beginners.[10] This gives some idea of the great interest which his treatise on the virtues held for the students and scholars of medieval Europe. The moral virtues provided Aquinas with a way to talk about a distinctively Christian teaching, namely, the universal call to holiness and beatitude. In the final analysis, Aquinas understands the practice of virtue as nothing less than the full realization of evangelical glory in this life. He held that the theology of the virtues, the gifts of the Holy Spirit, the beatitudes, and the fruits of Spirit together form a single instruction on Christian perfection.[11] Among other goals, the following pages help introduce the reader to the principal elements of this original synthesis of theological ethics.

The book comprises six chapters. The first chapter provides an introduction to the actual place which the moral virtues and virtue theory hold in contemporary theological ethics. Because the recent renewal of interest in the virtues originated largely among Anglo-American philosophers, the chapter first presents a brief survey of current work in philosophical ethics. Secondly, the chapter ponders the special conditions which Christian revelation imposes on the study of the virtues. This discussion leads to a consideration of realist moral theology. Indeed a leitmotif of the present work includes a conception of moral theology which depends principally on realist philosophy. In other words, moral theology must first of all recognize "the principles of the moral order which spring from human nature itself" as so many reflections of God's purposes and designs for the world—what Aquinas calls the Eternal Law. Likewise, although moral realism accords to human persons the highest dignity in the created order, it reserves to God the highest dignity simply speaking. Therefore, realist moral theology makes divine wisdom, not human reason, the ultimate measure of created morality, so that while right reason plays an important role in the development of a virtue-centered life, rationalizations about human conduct do not. Finally, in order to place a correct emphasis on the important matter of human autonomy, the chapter closes with a reflection on the dynamics of divine grace as they operate within the structure of our human psychology. Because I share St. Augustine's optimism about what the grace of Christ can accomplish in the life of an individual, I prefer to give an unequivocal priority to the workings of divine grace in those matters which pertain to eternal salvation, especially the moral life.

The second chapter treats a topic at once more specific and technical, namely, the theme of *habitus*. Aristotle bequeathed the concept to Western theology when he spoke about *hexis* and character in the *Nicomachean Ethics*. Subsequently, Aquinas and the schoolmen produced a richly developed instruction on this important element of human psychology. Virtue falls within the genus of *habitus*. The Thomist tradition, in particular, established a theological context for *habitus,* relating it at once to the *kenosis* of Christ and the metaphysics of created potency and act. After defining the precise nature of a *habitus,* chapter two explains the relationship between *habitus* and free choice. A description of how *habitus* operate as well as their principal characteristics completes the introductory material for the study of the virtues.

Since it presents a definition of moral virtue, chapter three brings the discussion to its focal point. First of all, the chapter considers the particular features of theological ethics which provide the framework for a general theory of the moral virtues. Because we define the moral virtues as good, operative *habitus,* it remains incumbent upon the moral realist to explain the term of the operation which virtue renders prompt, easy, and joyful. For the Christian believer, there exists but one ultimate goal, namely, that beatitude to which Christ welcomes the wise virgins. But our movement towards that beatitude requires the attainment of those created goods which human life needs for its proper perfection. In order to show how the moral virtues both perfect nature and ready us for beatitude, the chapter considers the exact nature of a moral virtue and the important elements of its definition. Chapter three then explores the different capacities of the human person which are capable of virtuous development: the intellect, the rational appetite, and the sense appetites. The question of virtue and emotion raises important issues in several fields of scientific inquiry. In an attempt to cast some light on matters oftentimes gravely misunderstood, I weigh some of the implications which Christian belief holds for those who experience the tugs and the pulls of disordered emotions. In short, moral realism shares St. Augustine's convictions concerning the rhythm of Christian life: it is Christ who overlooks sin, it is Christ who urges our conversion, and it is Christ who faithfully rewards perseverance in doing good.

The fourth chapter examines the central role which the virtue of prudence plays in the moral life. Until recently, the establishment of casuistry so disformed the moral topography that few, if any, Christian believers comprehended the necessity of prudence for shaping the moral life. Even now when most persons think of prudence, they associate the virtue with circumspection, foresight, or a kind of sharp intuition about how to proceed with the affairs of everyday life. Ordinarily, Christians consider conscience a far more important factor in the moral life than the virtue of prudence. As a result, we experience today a considerable amount of intellectual cacophony when theologians advance certain views which concern the "rights" of an individual's conscience. At the same time, we also witness the reaction which occurs when the Holy Father and the bishops rightly insist that the ordinary Magisterium of the

Church suffices for that religious submission of heart and mind required of the Christian faithful in moral matters. Such a state of affairs reflects ill on the unity which should exist within the Church of Christ. The virtue of prudence, on the other hand, supposes compatibility between freedom and authority.

Accordingly, chapter four explains that moral realism respects legitimate authority, i.e., the lawmaker, as an appropriate exponent of right reason. The virtue of prudence ensures that there exists between the intelligence of the moral agent and the truth of the moral law an authentic and intrinsic conformity. Moreover, this conformity alone avoids the conflicts which otherwise arise when the self-reliant individual judges the pronouncements of legitimate moral authority unrealistic and, therefore, considers exemption from them justifiable. The fourth chapter also elaborates how the intellectual virtue of prudence informs the other moral virtues so that the intellectual and affective movements of an individual resolve into a harmonized pattern of virtuous action. The unitive function of prudence characterizes moral realism as a unique and distinctive system of theological ethics. The chapter closes with an analysis of a prudential act and its three principal moments, namely, counsel, judgment, and command. To sum up, Christian prudence ensures that we act in conformity with the directives of right reason. While these find their principal historical exposition in Christian moral wisdom and the magisterial tradition of the Church, the designs and providence of the Eternal Law remain the unmeasured measure of the virtuous conduct which prudence imperates.

The fifth chapter turns our attention to the question of the development of the virtues. Of course, growth in virtue provides the opportunity for a range of different specialists to deliberate questions which pertain to human maturation and development. The perspective of this chapter remains strictly theological, even if Christian theology traditionally considers both the acquired and infused virtues. First of all, then, chapter five examines the way in which theologians speak about what causes the acquired virtues to develop in a given individual. But the chapter is mainly concerned about growth in virtue as the work of divine grace. The dynamic interplay which exists between the exercise of the acquired and the enjoyment of the infused virtues furnishes moral realism with a distinctive theory concerning the development of the virtuous life. In general, contemporary theologians prefer to consider only the infused virtues, that is, those qualities of Christian life which function in the believer actively united with Christ. On the other hand, some ethical autonomists even question whether any specifically Christian virtues exist. But moral realism recognizes both the givens of human psychology and, at the same time, the special prerogatives which belong to those who enjoy the benefit of divine friendship. Because the matter bears such great importance for pastoral ministry, the discussion in chapter five provides some of the most important distinctions and clarifications which a study of the moral virtues and theological ethics can provide for those who accept the Gospel.

The sixth and final chapter treats the principal characteristics which accompany the development of the virtues in an individual. Discussion of these properties, such as the mean, the connection, and the equality of the moral virtues, approximate teachings found in non-Christian authors, but these same topics also illustrate theses on the moral virtues held by patristic authors, whose Christian exegesis makes a difference in the interpretation of these well-established themes. A Christian view of the characteristics of the virtuous life includes the testimony which derives from the grace of Christ and the power of the Holy Spirit. In this context, the chapter also considers the celebrated adage that virtue abides in the middle—*virtus in medio stat*. All in all, the chapter offers an account of everyday examples which demonstrate how one who practices the moral virtues thereby develops a complete life in the Holy Spirit.

To sum up, the six chapters which comprise this volume on the moral virtues exhibit a specific order: First, an introduction to the present state of virtue theory in contemporary theology; second, technical information on the classical category for virtue, *habitus;* third, the definition of a moral virtue and the description of how it benefits our psychological capacities; fourth, the preeminent case of prudence and its unitive function in the moral life; fifth, discussion about what causes the moral virtues to grow according to nature and grace; and, sixth, the distinctive characteristics which accompany the life of virtue. The reader who studies this text will be ready to make a detailed examination of any one of the moral virtues. Like so many students of theological ethics in the past have done, one might choose, for example, to rummage through the *secunda pars* of Aquinas's *Summa theologiae.* More importantly, however, the book aims to introduce a view of the moral life which encourages the Christian believer to exercise the kind of moral vigilance which Jesus counsels in the parable of the wise and foolish maidens: "Afterward the other maidens came also, saying, 'Lord, lord, open to us'. But he replied, 'Truly, I say to you, I do not know you.' Watch therefore, for you know neither the day nor the hour" (Mt 25:11–13). St. Augustine puts further perspective on the need for this vigilance when he insists: "What if virtue leads us to a happy life, I would rather regard virtue as nothing at all, unless it also led to the highest love of God."[12]

1. THE MORAL VIRTUES AND CHRISTIAN FAITH

ISSUES IN PHILOSOPHY AND THEOLOGY

The present relevance which Aristotelian ethics holds for Christian moral theology derives in large measure from breakthroughs in British scholarship within the analytical tradition.[1] Peter Geach, for instance, provides a complete account of classical virtue theory in his small book, *The Virtues*,[2] treating the four cardinal virtues—prudence, justice, fortitude, and temperance—as well as the three theological virtues— faith, hope, and charity. Notwithstanding the inclusion of the theological virtues, Geach's work remains a philosophical text. "Faith is God's gift," he writes, "I try here only to remove obstacles to faith."[3] A bona fide theological text must aspire to do more than simply remove rational objections to revealed truth. If theology is to remain true to its character as a holy teaching, a *sacra doctrina,* its practitioners should ensure that every element of the instruction proceeds from and depends upon revealed wisdom. This standard applies equally to both moral theology and what we have become accustomed to call dogmatic theology.[4]

It remains a safe generalization to say that virtue theory occupies small place in the current renewal of moral theology, at least in Roman Catholic circles.[5] Of course, developments in philosophy usually require some time to influence theological discussion. Still, it is useful to inquire why the virtue tradition that once dominated so much of Christian thinking on moral matters scarcely receives attention today, even from those whose stated purpose includes the revision of Roman Catholic moral theory and practice.

Consider how Thomas Aquinas planned his treatment of "moral matter" in the *Summa theologiae*. "After a general consideration of virtues and vices and other points pertaining to moral matter in general," he writes in the prologue to the *secunda secundae*, "it is necessary to consider each of these one by one."[6] Aquinas devoted more space to the virtues, gifts, and beatitudes than to any other single topic in his textbook for beginners in theology, yet today few people would recognize these tractates as part of moral theology. When theologians debate such basic issues as the mode in which theology depends upon divine revelation and faith and no clear agreement exists even about theological method, it is not surprising to discover that moral theologians generally have chosen to ignore the precedent set by Aquinas and other medieval authors when they developed their moral theories within a framework of virtues and vices.

Today, efforts to revise moral theology often employ ethical models based upon divine command or rule theories, usually moderated by the principle of proportionate reason. Admittedly, the meanings and functions of "proportion" differ according to the usage of the various authors. Still, in the final analysis, proportionalist authors identify the moral life with ethical obligations concretized in norms or precepts, although, as is well known, they have relaxed the rigid moral legalism which the various systems of moral casuistry had highly developed. Casuistry refers to the kind of moral argument which dominated Roman Catholic theology for nearly four hundred years before the Second Vatican Council. Since revisionist moral theologians want to distance themselves from a narrow view of moral law, they recommend moral regulations with a certain flexibility depending on such factors as the weighing of results, the urgency of a particular situation, or the establishment of a hierarchy of moral values.[7] Self-determination and even imagination figure prominently in the way many moral theologians work out theories for decision making. Whatever success these techniques may promise for solving difficult cases of conscience, such trends offer little hope for restoring virtue to the place it should maintain in Christian moral theory.

Curiously, there does exist a similarity between the project of revisionist moral theologians and that of the earlier casuistry: both have shown little more than passing interest in the place of virtue in the moral life. As shown by the Belgian theologian Servais Pinckaers,[8] casuistry rejected the optimistic program set forth by such high medieval theologians as Aquinas. In his *Summa theologiae* Aquinas proposed to devote a tractate in turn to "each virtue, the gift corresponding to it, and the vices opposed to it." In this way, he insisted, "the whole of moral matter is placed in the context of the virtues," and so "nothing in morals will be overlooked."[9] Instead of this program, the casuist moral theologians conceived a highly juridical moral theology, one in which sin, conscience, the obligation to obey, and the moral law comprised the principal working elements. Accordingly, the casuist conception of morality sanctioned a conscientious observance of the moral law, i.e., the Decalogue and positive ecclesiastical legislation, as the principal standard for the moral life. Because the casuist authors developed their method by writing opinions on individual moral cases (hence the term *casuistry* from the Latin *casus [conscientiae]*), casuistry produced its own body of jurisprudence for moral matters.

A *complete* moral theory must certainly take account of individual cases. Aquinas himself emphasized the fact that moral argumentation becomes less useful precisely as it embraces a higher degree of universality.[10] Even so, he was able to elaborate a moral teaching that provided a full account of how right moral reason, ultimately derived from the highest and most universal wisdom, the *lex aeterna,* actually informed a person's most particular and individual actions.[11] He did this without primary recourse to authoritative interpretations of moral codes or other juridical ways of legislating morality. Aquinas recognized that these latter methods run the risk of emptying the New Law of its original force, the interior anointing by the Holy Spirit given to each believer in baptism. Perhaps no other factor more influences Aquinas's decision to develop an intrinsic morality than his convictions about what distinguishes the morality of the Christian dispensation from the Old Law of fear and works. His own words best express this crucial point with respect to the virtues. In his treatise on the New Law of grace, Aquinas writes:

> All the differences which are proposed between the New Law and the Old rest on the difference between what is perfect and what is imperfect. For the precepts of any law are given in view of the active exercise of moral virtues. Now imperfect men, who do not yet have the stable *habitus* of virtue, are drawn to the exercise of the virtues in a different way from those who are perfect in virtue. For those who do not yet have the stable *habitus* of virtue are drawn to the exercise of virtue by some extrinsic motive, e.g. the threat of penalties, or the promise of external rewards such as honor or riches and so on. And therefore the Old Law, which was given to the imperfect, i.e. those who have not yet obtained spiritual grace, was called the law of fear, inasmuch as it induced men to observe its precepts by the threat of various penalties; and it is said to contain various temporal promises. Those on the other hand who have moral virtue are drawn to the exercise of virtuous actions for the love of virtue, not on account of some external penalty or reward. And so the New Law, consisting primarily in spiritual grace itself implanted in men's hearts, is called the law of love; and it is said to contain spiritual and eternal promises, which are the objects of virtue,

especially charity. And so men are drawn to them intrinsically, not as to what is external to them but as to what is their very own. This too is why the Old Law is said to restrain the hand, not the mind since someone who abstains from sin through fear of a penalty does not simply speaking withhold his consent to sin, as does someone who abstains from sin for love of justice. And for this reason the New Law, which is the law of love, is said to restrain the mind.[12]

Such insistence on the interiority of the moral life provides the principal characteristic of a Christian virtue-centered morality, namely, that theological ethics must first affirm the transformation of the believer by grace, and then set forth the canons for virtuous conduct. "In the same way," writes St. Augustine, "God, who is the light of the inner self, aids the weakness of our spirit in order that we may do good, not in light of our justice but of his."[13]

Philosophers are accustomed to speak about what constitutes a perfection of nature; indeed, they enjoy talking about human existence. When philosophers consider the problem of what constitutes human perfection, they seek to describe the fulfillment of human life, that is, a good and happy life bringing delight to those who apprehend it. But moral theologians must also engage in the dialogue, since they alone can account for what gives perfect human form to the image of God. "It is the interior Master who instructs," affirms St. Augustine, "it is Christ who instructs."[14] If morality were only a matter of acting in conformity to a rule, one might argue that, even for the Christian, due observance of authoritative teaching would alone suffice to accomplish the purposes of a moral life. Yet such a limited view surely falls short of fully expressing that love which animates the New Law of interior grace. Moreover, simply to obey a moral rule cannot effect the radical transformation in a human person which the Christian life seeks to accomplish in us. As the New Testament clearly teaches, the mere observance of a moral precept can even frustrate the designs of divine love. "But woe to you Pharisees! for you tithe mint and rue and every herb, and neglect justice and the love of God; these you ought to have done, without neglecting the others" (Lk 11:42).

Ever since Elizabeth Anscombe, in her classic article, "Modern Moral Philosophy," brought the concept of "human flourishing" to the attention of moralists, Anglo-American philosophers, long anesthetized by Hume's declaration to the contrary, have been forced to take account of the relationship between ethics and anthropology.[15] The serious development of a virtue-centered morality requires some agreement about the essentials of human nature, towards the shaping of which virtue tends. At this time, as the diversity of opinion among authors amply demonstrates, philosophy remains hard pressed to reach agreement on what constitutes a normative human character.[16] Still, the theologian can promote such agreement. Arguably, a normative anthropology must, at least, remain open to what revelation discloses about human nature. Of course, no philosopher can declare, as the Church in fact does, that man is "the only creature on earth that God has wanted for its own sake."[17]

Central to a theological view of the human person, such as set forth in the doctrine of the *imago Dei,* remains the faith-affirmation that the ultimate destiny of each individual lies in beatific fellowship or union with the blessed Trinity. Admittedly, the fact that God remains our final goal does not provide immediate responses to the complicated ethical questions that arise in the course of a lifetime. But the vocation of each human person to participate in the beatific vision does significantly influence the work of the moral theologian. Skepticism about the role that God plays in the difficulties of everyday life, as agnostic existentialist philosophy reminds us, remains a consistent challenge to the specifically Christian doctrine of divine Providence. Still, a confident and accurate theological anthropology does provide a foundation for the establishment of an authentic theological ethics. Philosophical agnosticism about what constitutes human nature or its destiny need not undermine the task of elaborating a virtue-centered moral theology. In fact, some argue that we can only discover a comprehensive list of the created goods which compose human flourishing under the guidance of Christian revelation.[18]

VIRTUES AND THE GOSPEL

The Second Vatican Council's Decree on Priestly Formation called for a renewal of moral theology as "nourished by scriptural teaching."[19] Only such a program can serve the requirements of a moral theology that takes full account of the graced transformation of the human person taught by the New Testament authors. Even classical writers, such as Aristotle, advanced the view that moral virtue effects a qualitative change in both the person who possesses the particular virtue as well as in the action performed by the virtuous one.[20] More importantly both patristic and medieval theologians operated from the assumption that infused virtue effected a personal transformation in the believer.[21] One can easily observe the affinities which exist between this classical view of virtue and what the author of the letter to the Colossians had in mind when he wrote:

> Put to death therefore what is earthly in you: fornication, impurity, passion, evil desire, and covetousness, which is idolatry. On account of these the wrath of God is coming. In these you once walked, when you lived in them. But now put them all away: anger, wrath, malice, slander, and foul talk from your mouth. Do not lie to one another, seeing that you have put off the old nature with its practices and have put on the new nature, which is being renewed in knowledge after the image of its creator. (Col 3:5–10)

Yet, unfortunately, many of those who gave serious attention to the renewal mandated by the conciliar instruction looked elsewhere than to virtue theory for a model for constructing the new biblical morality.

Controversies about the authority which the sacred scriptures possess in moral argumentation arose. Earlier, the nineteenth-century English utilitarian Henry Sidgwick, whose opinion on this matter now is recognized as prototypical, held that the Bible provides no more definitive teaching in morals than the reasoning supplied by Plato or Aristotle.[22] But the monuments to Christian culture, such as the renowned mosaics in the baptistery at Florence, witness to a long tradition in which the Bible served as an instrument of specific instruction in Christian morals. Today theologians freely express misgivings about the use of the sacred scriptures to disclose specific moral truth, and they prefer instead to talk simply about methods of imaginative entry into the biblical texts.[23] This results in the frustration of the Council's plea for a scripture-based renewal of moral theology.

There are other reasons that account for the reluctance which theologians have shown towards launching a renewal of virtue theory. First, classical virtue theories depend to a considerable degree upon the work of ancient and, therefore, non-Christian philosophy. For example, Aristotle's *Nicomachean* and *Eudemian Ethics* served as principal philosophical source materials for Christian theologians in developing an adequate notion of virtue in moral theology.[24] Such a heavy reliance on non-Christian authors appears to run counter to the Council's directive for renewal from scriptural sources. On the other hand, the Book of Wisdom 8:7 affirms that divine wisdom "teaches self-control and prudence, justice and courage," and Christian authors as early as St. Ambrose found the same cardinal virtues proposed by classical philosophy to be a suitable starting point for describing an authentically Christian life.

Neglect of virtue in post-conciliar moral theology also derives from an alleged individualism inherent in virtue-centered theories. Admittedly, Aristotle states at the start of the *Nicomachean Ethics* that the principal concern of the virtuous person remains the pursuit of happiness. Similarly, Aquinas affirms early in the *secunda pars* of his *Summa theologiae* that final perfection for each individual rests in a personal vision of the Godhead. Still, these affirmations do not amount to an unqualified endorsement of ethics, whether philosophical or theological, as a solitary adventure, nor do they exclude its social dimension. On the contrary, good arguments can be developed to show that the virtuous shaping of an individual's character directly affects the well-being of the whole community. As long as Aristotle contends that "the human good turns out to be the soul's activity that expresses virtue,"[25] the exercise of the moral virtues inescapably brings the person into relationship with others. This happens either directly, as in the obvious case of justice, or indirectly, as when others benefit from one who possesses the virtues of personal discipline, temperance, and fortitude. For theological ethics, there exists a general, but real, sense in which every virtue remains ordered to the kind of social communication which befits the unity of believers in Christ. "For the whole law is fulfilled in one word, 'You shall love your neighbor as yourself'. But if you bite and devour one another take heed that you are not consumed by one another" (Gal 5:14,15).

Still another objection raises the issue of whether a virtue-centered morality concentrates too exclusively on the development of one's natural endowments. The exercise of moral virtue suggests the ethical counterpart of athletic training. (Aristotle actually refers to the practices of the Greek athletes at Olympia when discussing moral discipline.) In other words, to cultivate virtue presents the occasion for still another form of self preoccupation. Likewise, theologians allege that Thomist virtue theory runs the un-Christian risk of portraying the virtuous individual as one concerned principally with himself or herself. Is this a correct impression? Because Aquinas recognized the radical difference between the Old Law of self-reliance and the gratuity of the New Law, I think not. Christian theology understands the virtuous life as profoundly relational. On the other hand, self-regarding individualism does affect the actual situation of secular morality, as the sad issue of abortion clearly demonstrates. Those who support abortion frequently argue either along utilitarian lines, i.e., that some greater good will happen as a result, or in accord with the idealist vision, namely, that an individual—in this case the mother—possesses final and unmeasured control over her own person.

St. Thomas, however, recognized that the full development of true freedom and human flourishing requires a principle of rectitude. He called this rectitude *veritas vitae,* the truth of life, a sort of general virtue which undergirds all the other virtues and, in fact, the whole of human existence. "Truth of life, " he wrote, "is the kind of truth by which something exists as true, not by which someone speaks what is true. Like everything else one's life is called true on the basis of its reaching its rule and norm, namely divine law; by measuring up to this, a life has uprightness."[26] He goes on to assert that each specific virtue gives concrete expression to this general moral truthfulness. Only conformity to God's eternal plan for the world and for each individual person—what Aquinas calls *lex aeterna* or the Eternal Law—results in such a distinctively Christian way of life. As *Gaudium et spes* reminds us, the Church conceives no other ground for human community.[27]

For the Christian believer conformity to Christ in the Church of faith and sacraments provides the only legitimate way to attain the "truth of life." The conciliar documents repeatedly emphasize the centrality of Christ in salvation history. Admittedly, certain scholastic theologians, including Aquinas, developed their tractates on the virtues without prolonged and repeated reference to the uniquely Christian claim that moral perfection exists in anyone only to the extent that the person maintains a living relationship with Christ. In the case of Aquinas, the absence of frequent reference to Christ in the *secunda pars* happens simply because of his methodological presuppositions in developing the *Summa theologiae*.[28] Still, any theologian who fully grasps the New Testament teaching on the gratuity of divine grace realizes that every meritorious deed performed by the believer derives its efficacy from God's goodness. And Aquinas surely realized this happens only through the mediation of Jesus Christ. For Christ himself explicitly teaches this: "I am the true vine, and my Father is the vinedresser. . . . As the branch cannot bear fruit by itself, unless it abides in the vine, neither can you, unless you abide in me" (Jn 15:1,4).

REALIST MORAL THEOLOGY

One of the fundamental theses which guides the present discussion entails a particular view about the uniqueness of the Christian life. Theological ethicists debate how to distinguish the Christian moral life from whatever moral wisdom naked human nature and reason supply. A representative range of opinion includes, on the one hand, the humanist reduction of the content of all Christian moral instruction to whatever human reason renders available and, on the other hand, the fundamentalist restriction of all authentic moral teaching to whatever the New Testament expressly teaches. Some authors propose that Christian belief and hope merely provide a new style or motivation required to fulfill otherwise quite natural moral precepts.[29] Still others suggest that the principal difference between Christian and natural morality lies in the former's theological investment in a sacramental system with its own set of rules and obligations.[30] None of these views, however, provides a satisfactory description of the relationship which exists between moral philosophy and theological ethics nor an adequate account of the distinctive character of New Testament existence.

Rather, the familiar scholastic adage, *gratia perficit naturam*, grace perfects that nature which it embraces, provides the *point de départ* for a correct view of the relationship between Christian belief and moral conduct. Although subject to countless misinterpretations and, therefore, the beneficiary of unmerited deprecation, this principle holds a central place in the elaboration of a realist moral theology. It ensures that each of the principal moral virtues measures up to whatever a complete definition of virtue requires. Such a definition certainly includes what Aquinas calls "rectitudo appetitus."[31] A rectified appetite means that our emotional and appetitive capacities remain suitably disposed to achieve their proper goals or ends. Peter Geach has underscored the importance these goals or ends play in moral theory: "A moral code 'freely adopted' that ignores the built-in teleologies of human nature can only lead to disaster."[32] The perfecting of our human potential means, at least in part, that grace respects the built-in teleologies of human nature. Such a conformity of appetites to ends requires the work of intelligence as well. Neither the rational appetite, the will, nor the sense appetites, the concupiscible and irascible emotions, possess the ability to effect such a conformity in themselves. Accordingly, the cardinal virtues include the intellectual virtue of prudence, for only this virtue can assure that the *lex aeterna*, God's particular wisdom for the creature, duly informs each just, brave, and temperate action through the medium of correct moral reasoning.

The formal principle of virtue, realized in each of the cardinal virtues, remains the execution and pursuit of the reasonable good as God intends it. Human existence offers countless ways in which the reasonable good can be achieved. Thus, related to each of the cardinal virtues there exist specific virtues ordered to the realization of the definite and concrete goods that comprise the complete perfection of the human person. But this discussion proceeds from the starting point of Christian faith and commitment, so that each of these moral virtues contributes to the up-building of the believer's life. For the Christian the ultimate reasonable good remains the achievement of the goal which Paul announces to Titus: "For the grace of God has appeared for the salvation of all people, training us to renounce irreligion and worldly passions, and to live sober, upright, and godly lives in this world, awaiting our blessed hope, the appearing of the glory of our great God and Savior Jesus Christ" (Ti 2: 11–13). Moreover, the New Testament authors make it remarkably clear that Christian existence constitutes an entirely new way of life for the one who accepts the Christian dispensation.

This transformation that takes place in the believer makes sense only if Christian conversion entails an actual movement from one point to another point. Perhaps an example from philosophy might illustrate this important axiom about Christian development. Aristotle defined motion as the entelechy, i.e., the act, of that which exists in potency insofar as it is such.[33] To the extent that the act of faith, perfected by sacramental baptism, constitutes such an entelechy or action on the part of the believer, it entails a movement from the potential state of not-being-in-Christ to the actual state of being-in-Christ. In like manner, the moral life—the actual exercise of the moral virtues—reflects this same dynamic. This means that Christian maturation always exists in a state at once both relatively perfect and, at the same time, incomplete. Why? Because even in the baptized, i.e., those who are actually conformed to Christ and who confess their faith, there continues to exist a state of potential with respect to full conformity to the Risen Christ. St. Paul recognized this when he wrote to the Galatians: "My little children, with whom I am again in travail until Christ be formed in you!" (Gal 4:19). One might question whether anyone, even a saint, achieves this fullness of Christian maturity in this life.

Christian life, in order to remain a vital activity, must allow for development. The behavioral sciences have contributed a great deal to our understanding of the factors involved in human psychological development and, as a result, theologians willingly describe various patterns for growth in the spiritual life and freely provide appropriate counsel towards realization of Christian maturity. Some writers even borrow from the practices of world religions, for example, Sufi mysticism, in order to provide the models for these Christianized forms of psychotherapy.[34] Such experiments may be considered as an attempt to continue a long tradition of Christian effort aimed at developing authentic tools of spiritual guidance and direction. However, in order to ensure that they achieve the goal of furthering the soul's union with God, these methods require theological surveillance.[35] In the same way, classic spiritual theology possessed its own psychological models for guiding the spiritual development of those eager for a deeper share in the riches of Christ.

However, everyone engaged in the theological project does not share the perspectives of realist moral theology. Certain authors within the Christian tradition hold the view that Christian growth entails simply the unfolding of an increasingly more intense manifestation of the divine Spirit perennially active in the world. Karl Rahner, for example, sets the theoretical underpinnings for this view by his celebrated doctrine of a "supernatural existential." "In the concrete, then, there remains no other conceivable possibility but a faith which is simply the obedient acceptance of man's supernaturally elevated self-transcendence, the obedient acceptance of his transcendental orientation to the God of eternal life."[36] To be sure, Rahner maintains the traditional Christian doctrine on God's absolute freedom with respect to anything which falls outside the divine nature. Still, many have interpreted his work to imply that

Christian theology and ethics should avoid any talk about the human reality outside the context of the person's supernaturally elevated transcendentality. Such a course can leave the question of growth in virtue at least ambiguous.

During the middle decades of the twentieth century, theologians debated, often sharply, the proper ways to express the relationship between nature and supernature.[37] No conclusive agreements were reached, although ecclesiastical authority did intervene to moderate one or another of the less nuanced positions. Rahner's views should not be counted among these latter. Nevertheless, despite the broad variety of moral codes which exist among peoples, many share the view that some authentic theological meaning can be found in the phrase "anonymous Christian." Some carefully crafted distinction may render this concept useful for Christian theology.[38] Still, one hesitates in face of Rahner's declaration that "to be a Christian is simply to be a human being, and one who also knows that this life which he is living, and which he is consciously living, can also be lived even by a person who is not a Christian explicitly and does not know in a reflexive way that he is a Christian."[39] Such a claim somehow seems alien to the authentic Christian tradition. How does such optimism about the human condition stand alongside St. Paul's candid determination on the importance of the moral law?

> Now we know that the law is good, if any one uses it lawfully, understanding this, that the law is not laid down for the just but for the lawless and disobedient, for the ungodly and sinners, for the unholy and profane, for murders of fathers and murders of mothers, for manslayers, immoral persons, sodomites, kidnappers, liars, perjurers, and whatever else is contrary to sound doctrine, in accordance with the glorious gospel of the blessed God with which I have been entrusted. (1 Tm 1:8–11)

Obviously, St. Paul considered the transformation which Christian conversion brings about in the moral life important enough to spell out the matter in explicit terms for the young apostle.

Much of contemporary moral theology reflects uncertainty about the essentials of Christian conversion. This results, in part, from a failure of certain moralists to grasp how little German transcendental philosophy interests itself in what accounts for the fact that something moves from one point to another. Rahner "can readily say that the ultimate and most specific thing about Christian existence consists in the fact that a Christian allows himself to fall into the mystery which we call God."[40] But how can such an experience illuminate the progressive transformation of one's moral conduct by divine grace? The virtue theory presented in this book seeks to clarify the question of transformation by investigating the relationship between a life lived according to human resources and the new life of grace and Christian faith. Central to this conception of the moral virtues lies the conviction that God does change us. Consider St. Paul's confident appraisal of the outcome of Christian conversion: "For as many of you as were baptized into Christ have put on Christ. There is neither Jew nor Greek, there is neither slave nor free, there is neither male nor female: for you are all one in Christ Jesus" (Gal 3:27,28).

The medieval tradition of natural law also illumines the character of a moral life based upon the exercise of *recta ratio*, right reason, yet open to "put on" Christ. Although authors place different emphases in describing the ways natural law concretely operates in human life, the common tradition propounds one specific point, namely, that human nature does provide a basis for elaborating an authentic morality. Both friends and foes of natural law theory risk a serious error of interpretation when they seek to identify natural law morality as a complete, self-sustaining moral theory. Frequently, negative reaction to natural law arises from the suspicion that those who theologize about natural moral law in fact wish to make a metaphysical biology the equivalent of the Christian dispensation. Or, natural law adversaries allege that giving serious consideration to the place natural law holds in Christian morals reduces the distinctive gift of grace to something extrinsic and, therefore, apparently dispensable for the Christian life. The present construal of natural law pursues neither of these directions.[41] All in all, natural law plays an important, but limited, role in realist moral theology.

In order to develop a realist moral theology, the theologian must take seriously the doctrine of creation. It remains possible to recognize the aptitudinal image of God in every human creature without thereby affirming that special divine presence which theologians refer to as sanctifying grace. Aquinas correctly pointed out that the original Godly image in man and woman established by the divine word of creation differs from the restoration of that same image accomplished by the incarnate Son through the power of the Holy Spirit. The moral theologian must examine natural law inclinations and the human virtues as part of the more specific effort to uncover the full intelligibility of Christian life. Realist moral theology, especially when it discusses the moral virtues, seeks to explain how grace perfects nature: *gratia perficit naturam*. Whatever help realist moral philosophy provides will be welcomed as an indispensable aid to such theological reflection. For "here there cannot be Greek and Jew, circumcised and uncircumcised, barbarian, Scythian, slave, free man, but Christ is all, and in all" (Col 3:11).

HUMAN PSYCHOLOGY AND GOSPEL GRACE

The patristic authors, well disposed towards supplying persuasive arguments for the legitimacy of Christian wisdom, offer a remarkable synthesis of Christian doctrine and practical moral teaching. Among the central concerns of the Fathers of the Church we find the need to provide solid moral instruction for those newly converted to the Christian Gospel. Often such instruction included applications of the two great commandments Jesus announces in the Gospel: "You shall love the Lord your God with all your heart, and with all your soul, and with all your strength, and with all your mind; and your neighbor as yourself" (Lk 10:27). No Church Father ever conceived that the love of which Jesus speaks amounted to a merely natural love, one which arose out of our personal energies and resources. Rather, each understood that Christian love originates in the very power of the New Law itself. Thus, they interpreted well St. Paul's teaching, "When we cry, 'Abba! Father!' it is the Spirit himself bearing witness with our spirit that we are children of God" (Rom 8:15,16), and affirmed that the divine energy informs the Christian believer's every action. And though the anti-Pelagian tracts of St. Augustine did argue against the view that the Christian life amounts simply to a human life lived in a world generally transformed by grace, still the patristic authors did not engage in much speculation as to how one might distinguish the human and divine elements in the moral life.

The teaching of the second chapter of the Letter to the Romans influenced both patristic and medieval thinkers in their understanding of the existence of a moral instruction other than the one announced by Jesus Christ. "When Gentiles," wrote St. Paul, "who have not the law do by nature what the law requires, they are a law unto themselves, even though they do not have the law" (Rom 2:14). But the inability of this moral law written on the heart to achieve its own fulfillment impressed the earliest Christian thinkers. Like good apologists, they argued for the importance of accepting the Christian Gospel on the basis that such belief alone enabled the person of good will to fulfill even the precepts of a natural moral code. Aquinas reflects this understanding in his *Summa theologiae* when, in a remarkably balanced reply to the question whether an individual can will and do good without grace, he answers that although an individual may successfully perform certain authentically human actions apart from divine assistance, one in such a state cannot perform the whole good which is connatural to human flourishing, so as to fall short in nothing. Aquinas then employs a medical metaphor to make his point. "So a sick man is capable of some movement by himself, yet he cannot move perfectly with the movement of a healthy man unless he is healed by the aid of medicine."[42] This conclusion approximates the conclusion reached by St. Paul after his lengthy inquiry in Romans on the actual state of one who has been redeemed by the power of Christ. "We know that the whole creation has been groaning in travail together until now; and not only the creation, but we ourselves, who have the first fruits of the Spirit, groan inwardly as we wait for adoption as sons, the redemption of our bodies" (Rom 8:22,23).

This groaning, which St. Paul clearly presents as belonging to those earnest about living in accord with Christian perfection, suggests a fundamental tension in Christian life. This tension exists between what the Christian believer recognizes as part of the old self, "captive to the law of sin which dwells in the members," and the new self, set free from all of that by the power of the Spirit in the risen Christ. The medieval theologians explained how this tension can contribute to growth in Christian virtue. Aquinas argued that the reason why disordered sensuality is not entirely cured in this life reflects divine wisdom itself. "Infirmity remains in us after baptism, just as a wise physician discharges a patient without having cured his illness if it could not be cured without the danger of a more serious illness."[43] In other words, growth in Christian living always requires the frank recognition that we stand in potential to further conformity to Christ. Refusal to acknowledge our sinfulness amounts to a form of disordered pride, as Aquinas's reference to a "more serious illness" makes clear.

At the same time, this tension reminds us that the Christian life, in order to attain its goal, requires the expenditure of personal energy. The history of theology recurrently manifests a marked division of opinion among theologians as to what constitutes the proper relationship between divine grace and human effort in the accomplishment of a morally good action or series of actions. However, these debates cannot distract our attention at this moment.[44] The recognition that, as Lactantius put it, "virtue consists not in knowing the good and the evil but, rather, in doing the good and avoiding the evil,"[45] points up the importance of attending to the thoroughly practical side of Christian life. Gospel pragmatism requires this.

The practice of virtue requires a proper knowledge of the goods which a virtuous life seeks to attain. Aristotle stressed the importance knowledge of ends plays in determining practical wisdom: "Then surely knowledge of this [highest] good is also of great importance for the conduct of our lives, and if, like archers, we have a target to aim at, we are more likely to hit the right mark."[46] Theological ethics must give the same attention to the established goods of human life—"the built-in teleologies of human nature"— as it does to rational theories about what makes for a good life. This partially explains why Christian virtue theory traditionally welcomes moral wisdom even from outside the pages of the New Testament. Both St. Augustine and St. Ambrose knew that Plato mentions the cardinal virtues in *The Republic* (Bk.4, chap.6).[47] In an important moral textbook from the early Middle Ages, Gregory the Great provides a good example of the successful appropriation of classical learning which the Christian tradition made.[48]

The *Moralia*, Gregory's commentary on the Book of Job, provided a complete, systematic account of the virtues put at the service of Christian moral theology. Like so many others before him, Aquinas profited from this text. The Latin Western tradition, at least through the twelfth century, insisted that moral virtues remain firmly connected with the theological virtues of faith, hope, and charity. These distinguishing components of Christian moral life alone transform a philosophical doctrine into an authentic Christian moral teaching. Following this line of thought, Aquinas goes so far as to assert that the moral life remains radically incomplete unless the theological virtues of faith, hope, and charity render each person capable of working towards the distinctively Christian goal of ecclesial unity and, ultimately, of beatific union with God.[49]

However, to Aquinas's credit, he also maintains this position without adopting the radical Augustinian interpretation concerning charity's role in the Christian life. As a result, his moral theology shows a different temper from that developed by thinkers influenced exclusively by the texts of St. Augustine. These latter usually adopt a predictably negative stance when it comes to discussing the autonomous character of anything related to the Christian dispensation. Theologians of this Augustinian persuasion prefer, therefore, to identify the moral virtues as so many aspects of the single virtue of divine charity. Those who adopt such a position need not share the pessimistic view which schools of outermost Augustinianism espouse concerning abandoned human nature. On the contrary, their writings often produce limpid expositions of the peculiar values found in the New Testament and Christian spirituality. Nevertheless, as we shall see later, the identification of every aspect of the moral life with charity does result in certain consequences for moral theology.[50]

Aquinas does not accept this solution to the problem of elaborating a Christian moral teaching. Rather, he joins a number of thinkers who affirm that acquired virtue remains authentic virtue even when it exists in one who has accepted the Gospel's announcement of gratuitous salvation.[51] Theologians of this class share a common appreciation of the role that metaphysics can play in solving questions raised by theology. They introduce efficient causality in such a way so as to explain both the relationship between the acquired virtues and charity as well as to account for how one grows in the Christian life. They further em-

ploy final causality in order to describe the harmony between the finalities of human life and the ultimate Good of
Christian life. As a result, realist moral theology can present a view of the moral life as a true means towards the
achievement of beatitude, yet not engage in the moralizing
so often found among thinkers for whom virtues remain
simply instruments for acquiring merit or conditions for
gaining eternal life.

This study assumes that Aquinas made the right choice
in his response to the question: Can the theologian properly
consider the natural, acquired virtues even within the context of a theological ethics? As a result of Aquinas's positive
view on this matter, the following pages purport to sketch
the essential features of a practical theology, one which
attends to the workings of both nature and grace. *The
Moral Virtues and Theological Ethics* is meant for those
seeking to live in fellowship with "whatever is true, whatever is honorable, whatever is just, whatever is pure, whatever is lovely, whatever is gracious" (Phil 4:8). Because the
moral virtues embody just these biblical values, a discussion of their theology also serves to illumine the instruction
given by the Second Vatican Council's *Lumen gentium*: "In
order to reach this perfection, the faithful should use the
strength dealt out to them by Christ's gift, so that following
in his footsteps and conformed to his image, doing the will
of God in everything, they may wholeheartedly devote
themselves to the glory of God and to the service of their
neighbor."[52]

2. *HABITUS,* CHARACTER, AND GROWTH

HABITUS AND CHRISTIAN *KENOSIS*

Aristotle's account of *hexis,* especially in the *Nicomachean Ethics,* provided Christian theologians with some of the psychological undergirding required for a complete discussion of virtue theory.[1] Recently theologians of the reformed tradition, usually reluctant to employ non-biblical categories in theology, have come to accept the value of the concept for theological ethics.[2] While interpreters differ about the precise philosophical meaning Aristotle intended for this elusive reality, it is usually translated as a "state of character."[3] This concept goes far to guarantee a full measure of importance to the principal psychological capacities of human nature. As a result of the refinements which Christian philosophy gives to *hexis,* moral realism can emphasize the connection between how these capacities are formed in a given individual and what sort of behavior he or she will manifest.

By definition, *habitus,* to use the more familiar Latin term, embodies a definite ability for growth through activity.[4] The scholastic theologians understood the important function that *habitus* has in shaping human conduct. Accordingly, they described *habitus* as holding a middle position between potency—the capacity for action—and full actuality—actually doing something.[5] Voluntary activity, then, always remains a realization of one or another *habi-*

tus. A person without any *habitus* lacks what is required for sure comportment, and finds any kind of purposeful activity difficult and burdensome. Moreover, as long as our psychological capacities persist in this underdeveloped state, human potential goes unrealized.

Such a conception of *habitus* implies a dynamic view of the human person. Aristotle clearly identified the causal relationship between *habitus* and free choice (*prohairesis*).[6] Certain authors, however, failed to take proper account of Aquinas's explicit appropriation of this important feature of Aristotelian ethics,[7] and thus, the opinion that realist theology imprisons human nature in an abstract and inert shell enjoys a certain currency. But if one fully grasps the existentialist implications of the classical doctrine of *habitus* as Aquinas developed it, such a supposition finds little justification. The eighteenth-century British moralist Joseph Butler attests to a correct understanding of what *habitus* means for Christian life. In his Third Sermon at the Rolls Chapel, he says that "when virtue has become habitual, when the temper of it is acquired, what was before confinement ceases to be so, by becoming choice and delight."[8] Nevertheless, we find writers who still present the notion of *habitus* as nothing more than an acquired pattern of behavior which results, principally, from repeated actions of the same kind, like putting so many creases in a starched linen cloth.

Some moral theologians, unalerted to the dangers inherent in identifying morality with the merely habitual, concluded that *habitus* would serve nicely as a concept for training in morals. And philosophers can point to certain texts in Aristotle which lend support to this partial interpretation.[9] As the image of creased cloth suggests, these same theologians talk as if morality amounts simply to developing the proper routines of a Christian life, such as keeping the commandments. In order to underscore the gross misunderstanding implicit in this view, one contemporary theologian published an article, "Virtue is Not a

Habit,"[10] wherein he insisted that *habitus* in the authentic scholastic sense means, above all, openness to creative activity, not stilted repetition. Even so, the notion of *habitus* fell out of currency among post-conciliar theologians, who, seeing the dangers in presenting too mechanical a view of Christian growth,[11] rejected the concept as an unsuitable category for handling all that a fully personalist moral theology required.

Despite this general trend, other authors, especially from within the Thomist tradition, understood the advantage which a more sophisticated interpretation of *habitus* held out for moral theory.[12] *Habitus* supposes a conception of the human person as open to development and modification from both natural and divine causes. Furthermore, *habitus* points up the difference between what derives from authentically personal activity and what remains rooted in the biological givens of temperament or personality type. Aquinas himself clearly understood that each human person possessed certain natural endowments, as distinct from *habitus,* which establish, within the limits set by common nature, the range of expression achievable by personal effort. To take a simple example, the capacity for bravery common to all men and women develops one way in the soldier of fortune and another way in the person who, for reasons such as physical stature (which do not result from voluntary choosing), constitutionally shuns all physical conflict. Still, barring abnormal biological defect, each personality "type" possesses the radical capacity for developing the major *habitus* of action. In fact, *habitus* development can even compensate for natural imbalances in a person, for instance, when the soldier of fortune, having discovered the meaning of restraint, practices meekness.

In sum, a realist anthropology recognizes that this man or that woman, i.e., individual instances of human nature, exhibit different aptitudes for moral development. This recognition does not lead to Pascal's pessimistic observation, "Vérité au-deçà des Pyrénées, erreur au-delà"—What's true on one side of the Pyrenees is false on the other.[13] Why? The true distinction of the human person lies in the common inbred capacities proper to the species, even though each individual embodies these in different ways. Since this native potential originally exists in a pure state of indeterminacy, the same person experiences a certain poverty. As a result of this indeterminacy, the moral life involves an educative and developmental process. And the progress of virtue or the growth of vice depends upon how successfully an individual can modify these indeterminacies into qualities of excellence.

Given its charter as a divine science, Christian moral theology must seek to sound the harmonies that exist between human psychology and revealed truth. In his treatment of *habitus,* Aquinas was influenced by St. Augustine as well as by Aristotle and Averroës (these latter being the experimental psychologists of their respective periods in history).[14] On the other hand, faith can also cast an explanatory light onto matters of human science. Accordingly, the Christian moral theologian may choose to illumine the Aristotelian doctrine of *habitus* with a theological truth, such as the christological doctrine of *kenosis.* The New Testament reports that Christ "though he was in the form of God, did not count equality with God a thing to be grasped, but emptied himself, taking the form of a servant, being born in the likeness of men" (Phil 2: 6–7). Standard theological interpretation of this passage affirms that the Eternal Son, though maintaining his full divine status, accepted what alone remains impossible for God, the actual condition of possibility.[15] Christ did this inasmuch as he assumed a full and complete human nature and accepted the personal history implied in living out a human existence. In the case of Christ, meritorious acts of love and obedience form the center of his life of preeminent virtue. By this kind of life, ultimately expressed in his salvific death on the cross, Christ makes complete sanctification possible for the whole human race.

In order to make the comparison of this central New Testament doctrine with a *habitus,* it should be observed that the life of Christ the Head moves contrapuntally to that of those who are joined to him as members of his Body. For Christ, the movement entails abandonment of his divine prerogatives, although not his personal excellence as the Second Person of the blessed Trinity, and the taking on of every human deficiency compatible with the uniqueness of his divine personhood and mission. This *kenosis,* as the patristic writers remind us, allows Christ to embrace the salvific life and death which establishes once and for all the salvation of the human race. By contrast, the life of the believer begins in a state of natural *kenosis,* what amounts to the poverty of indeterminacy, and from there moves towards the perfections which constitute a virtuous moral life. All this follows a pattern of gradual, progressive development which evolves, above all, in accord with the providential dispositions of divine grace. The Christian faith maintains the unique claim that such moral development occurs only in the one who actively seeks continued conformity with Christ, who for our sakes took the form of a slave. The Eastern mystical tradition expresses it simply: "The eye cannot see without light; without Christ souls cannot have true life or peace."[16]

HABITUS AND PERSONALITY

As noted above, current theological use of *habitus* largely derives from certain remarks provided by Aristotle about *hexis.* Still, the *Nicomachean Ethics* contributes only one strand towards an intelligent theological appropriation of *habitus.* In addition, the findings of the behavioral sciences can provide valuable insights about character. Developmental psychology, in particular, defines itself as the study of factors which contribute to the shaping of an individual's traits. However, moral theology needs to raise a certain caution with respect to the empirical sciences, especially when it comes to employing their inferences concerning the human person. Behavioral scientists do not necessarily share the common and fundamental assumption about the spiritual character of the human person that is indispensable to an authentic Christian teaching. This difference, although not always made clearly explicit, especially when the results of scientific investigations are translated into popular form, remains highly significant. Christian theology can critically appropriate scientific findings, provided their underlying anthropological suppositions do not reduce the human individual to its material components or remain agnostic about the basic constitution or ultimate destiny of the human person.[17] The freedom and dignity of God's children surpass the limits established by all forms of psychological determinism.

Within its own framework, realist moral theology also seeks to explain how moral development affects the very constitution of the human person. The fact that *habitus* can radically modify the whole of a human person implies something about the metaphysical structure of a created nature. In particular, *habitus* exist only in creatures, for only created realities possess the capacity for such change and development. Human activity can only approximate a state of expunging all potentiality; it never achieves it. Undergirding this particular construal of creation and potentiality remains the distinction adopted by realist philosophers between essence and existence. Recall that classical theology recognizes pure actuality only in the divine nature, but not, as certain humanist philosophers hope, in homo sapiens.

Aquinas's discussion of acquired *habitus* rests on the conviction that human capacities develop precisely as a result of properly human activity, the synergy of free choice and intelligence. What is more, such development does not simply affect the way in which an individual acts, though it accomplishes that as well. Rather, action can account for change in the very reality of the self. In other words, actions change the individual. Christian doctrine asserts that the extent of the change can reach to the very core of a person's selfhood and identity. For example, the virtue of filial piety can effectively alter the rebellious and disaffected adolescent so that the young person becomes an honest and respectful member of the household.[18] Christian theology, supported by the New Testament's assertion of the radical power that grace holds out to the human person, supposes that such a virtuous transformation of the self can occur in many circumstances. *Habitus* provides the metaphysical basis for elaborating a moral theology confident enough of itself to give serious attention to this kind of personal transformation.

This explains why the scholastics, when asked to define *habitus,* chose to locate it within the philosophical category of quality. This third of the categories of being, one of a list of ten irreducible types of things drawn up by Aristotle, designates one of the ways a given substance becomes identified as a special, predicable kind of thing. Quality derives from an actual internal ordering or arrangement of the substance's parts. It makes things to be different in the way cold gruel is different from hot soup, a lame thoroughbred from a winning racehorse, or sweet candy from cane sugar. Quality does not amount simply to placing a thing within its proper classification or to an extrinsic, merely ephemeral modification of a subject. Quality means to possess oneself in a determined way. The Latin phrase, *se habere,* used by the commentators to distinguish this reflexive sense of "having" from its more usual transitive meaning, as in "to possess a thing," aptly points up the use intended by Aquinas. The theologian, when he speaks about *habitus* as a quality, understands that quality refers to a real modification of a person's moral character. Vicious *habitus* produce a vicious individual; virtuous *habitus,* a virtuous person.

As Aquinas points out in the case of one who merits capital punishment, vicious *habitus* formation in a given individual can reach a point where something of the excellence which belongs to human nature disappears.[19] On the other hand, the potentiality ingredient in each created nature argues for the possibility of renewed moral reform. (A state may make the political judgment, however, that circumstances do not allow for this, as in the case of treason during war or the killing of a prison guard.) Accordingly, Christian theology insists against the common tendency to suppose that patterns of sinful behavior, even when supported by repeated actions, definitively establish one's personal identity. Virtue makes a real saint, but vicious *habitus* leave the person in a state of disordered potential. At the same time, the conviction that *habitus* represents a genuine qualification of one's person—clinical psychologists may prefer to use the expression "personality" here—allows realist moral theology to affirm that the radical correction of moral disorders alway remains feasible.

Quality designates a progressive appreciation or depreciation of the moral capacities of the human person. St. Thomas will insist that for the quality to be described as a *habitus* it must attain a certain degree of permanence in an individual's human psychology. He distinguishes *habitus* from dispositions precisely on the basis of how easily the two kinds of qualification change.[20] Since the moral life requires free choice to develop, the measure or value of a given quality, that is, whether it embodies a virtue or a vice, will result from how well or ill such choice conforms to the requirements of authentic moral wisdom. The Eternal Law, *lex aeterna*, remains, then, the ultimate source and measure for evaluating the *habitus* which characterize a person. St. Paul witnesses to this basic Christian perspective when he reminds the Corinthians: "Therefore, if any one is in Christ, he is a new creation, the old has passed away, behold the new has come"(2 Cor 16:17). Of course, the veritable challenge of the Gospel consists in bringing people to trust that this kind of conversion remains open to everyone.

DEVELOPMENT OF *HABITUS*

During the Second World War, theologians such as Dietrich Bonhoeffer and others emphasized the right and obligation of individual Christians to place the dictates of conscience before conformity to what, at best, amounted to nominal Christianity. Although the ethics of responsibility underscores the radical demands of Gospel life, those who employ this model in theological ethics often find it difficult to incorporate *habitus* into their proposals. However this should not be the case as *habitus* actually facilitate the discharge of responsibility. Why? Because *habitus* provide the whole person with settled capacities for action which surpass the simple ability to exercise will power. In fact, one author describes *habitus* as "a metaphysical perfectant."[21] Such a perfection heightens our human capacities to such an extent that those who act with a "habituated" intellect, will, and appetites approach the optimum performance of the strongest and most perfect human being. This means that how a person knows (by the exercise of the mind or intellect), how a person loves (by the exercise of a free will or rational appetite), and how a person tempers sense-urges (which arise out of the emotions or sense appetites), in short, all characteristically human abilities require diverse *habitus* in order to function properly. Accordingly, rather than serve as an obstacle to the unfolding of authentic freedom and responsibility, *habitus* provide the indispensable matrix for realizing free and responsible Christian behavior.[22]

Since *habitus* remain ordered to action, they require certain particular conditions to develop. A power or capacity able to perform only one kind of action neither allows nor requires the formation of *habitus*. Rather, there must exist in the capactiy which develops a *habitus* the potential for diverse kinds of activity. This becomes evident when one considers that capacities which perform in only one way do so without the aid of training—nobody, for example, requires instruction in order to use the digestive system. But sailing a boat, since it involves capacities which could be developed for other activities, does require a *habitus*. Accordingly, *habitus* formation occurs only when there exists in a subject what the scholastic commentator Cajetan calls a "variety in parts."[23] In short, this means that a capacity enjoys the possibility for diverse kinds of actions. Unless a capacity can perform in many different ways, insists Aquinas, the human person need not acquire in that area of human ability whatever perfection *habitus* produces.[24]

Habitus development also requires another condition in the subject. Besides being capable of diverse realizations of activity, a capacity must also possess a certain malleability or suppleness as regards undergoing change. Since *habitus* shape activity, any psychological determination in a capacity inhibits the development of a *habitus*. For example, because we can only see colored objects, sight does not require a *habitus* of vision, but because we can choose to consume either good or bad foodstuffs, proper eating does require the development of *habitus*. The intrinsic relationship between the formation of *habitus* and the ability to exercise freely certain kinds of activity means that *habitus* can develop in the intellect, the will, and, to the extent that they follow right reason, the sense appetites.

Finally, *habitus* development does not take place in anyone without the exercise of some agency. Theological ethics must hold that *habitus* develop either as a result of human agency or, according to the teaching of the faith, as a result of divine benevolence. In the latter case, because they result directly from the power of the Holy Spirit, the *habitus* are called infused. Since the New Testament *kerygma* announces that divine grace effects a twofold change in creatures made after the image of God, infused *habitus* serve to elucidate the biblical doctrine of justification quite well. First, image-restoration consists in the rectification of disordered appetite. This constitutes, in effect, the breaking of old, vicious *habitus*. Second, image-perfection entails the acquisition of the whole panoply of graced-endowments. These include the *habitus* of the moral virtues, of the theological virtues, and of the gifts of the Holy Spirit as well as the enjoyment of the fruits of the Spirit and the practice of the beatitudes. For theological ethics, moral categories can only partially describe the perfection of Christian *habitus*, for those who develop the *habitus* of a just life as the New Testament depicts it attain a share in "the unsearchable riches of Christ" (Eph 3:8) himself.

3. WHAT IS A MORAL VIRTUE?

MORAL VIRTUE AND THE GOAL OF CHRISTIAN LIFE

When theological writers describe the Christian moral life as the gradual perfection of the image of God in the human person, they mirror the extensive treatment given to this subject by the Fathers of the Church.[1] St. Augustine, more than any other patristic author, explained the theological significance of the divine image in the human person. Especially did he appreciate the Trinitarian implications of this doctrine for human destiny.[2] The term or ultimate goal of human existence remains a personal union of the believer with God. Instead of a vision of the divine nature, theologians today prefer to speak about beatific fellowship with God. In either case, beatitude is seen as the final perfection of the Trinitarian indwelling initially established in each believer at baptism. More precisely, the Christian enjoys a personal relationship with each Person of the blessed Trinity, a relationship which begins in the life of faith on earth and reaches fulfillment in heaven. Despite the confusion this subject causes philosophers, theologians rightly insist that morally good human activity remains ordered towards the realization of this single supernatural goal.[3] This reflects another intuition of St. Augustine, that all true virtue leads to a love of the highest Good.

Such a conception of the moral life also explains why Aquinas made a point of situating his moral theology within the broader theological context of our supernatural destiny. He placed the Christian affirmation that the beatific vision serves as the ultimate destiny of each human person at the very start of his treatment of the moral life and virtues.[4] According to a principal postulate of the *Summa theologiae*, the human person stands between God as creative source and God as beatifying goal. As we shall see in a later chapter, to affirm that the whole moral life remains ordered to a goal that human resources alone cannot accomplish raises certain difficulties for Christian theology. This tenet implies more than the hope that those who lead morally good lives can expect a divine reward. Rather, the presence of the blessed Trinity in a Christian life of virtue profoundly alters the substance of a person's moral life. The moral theologian must address the concrete specifics entailed in virtuous living, even if only God can bestow on those predestined to eternal glory virtue's ultimate perfection.[5]

When Aquinas defined virtue as good operative *habitus*, he sought to emphasize, among other things, that virtue is productive of good ends.[6] Ordinarily philosophers evaluate *habitus* on the basis of the perfection which it achieves in human nature. Human nature refers to the form life takes in a human being; as embodied spirit, each person enjoys the powers of human life—the characteristic human abilities or capacities—as well as the exercise of these powers—human activity. A good *habitus* makes an agent tend to act in accordance with the agent's own nature, whereas a bad *habitus* makes the agent tend to act against the agent's nature.[7] Given the doctrine of the Trinitarian indwelling, for the Christian to exist in accord with his or her nature means concretely discovering the way towards God and the beatific union which constitutes eternal life. This does not mean that the life of virtue makes sense only within an eschatological framework as if heaven were simply a reward for right conduct. The virtue tradition in theological ethics deals with questions of this world, and the concrete ways which lead to God encompass everything which is part of human existence, with the result that virtue perfects every significant aspect of our lives.

Theologians also speak about virtue as *habitus* in order to identify certain qualities of action which belong to a life lived according to Christian virtue. In particular, authors point out three distinctive features of action qualified by *habitus*: First, promptness or readiness to do something; second, ease or facility in performing the action; third, joy or satisfaction while doing it.[8] These features indicate that virtue overcomes the radical indeterminacy present in the human person and develops a sort of second or new nature ordained to achieve the goals for which human life strives. "New nature" suggests the kind of transformation which grace accomplishes in the believer. The distinction some of the Church Fathers drew between the image of God and the likeness of God in the human creature illumines the role which virtue plays in the Christian life. Gregory of Nyssa wrote: "Likeness is the acquisition or progressive realization of the image; it is a striving for assimilation, a modeling of self according to the exigencies of the image, which God has deposited in us like some preliminary sketch."[9] On this account, the moral life describes a journey towards God in which the powers of a person are fully centered upon Christian happiness.

Although virtue disposes the Christian for right conduct, its development does not automatically eliminate conflict and struggle from the Christian life. As a matter of fact, it can happen that more than one *habitus* coexist in the same person. One *habitus* may lead a person to act in accord with a sense inclination, for example, the man who smokes one cigarette after another. At the same time, another *habitus* can incline him to act in accordance with his higher nature. (For the philosopher, higher nature in this context could refer only to human intelligence.) If the smoker accepted conclusive evidence that his smoking would inevitably result in a certain infirmity, a *habitus* of the higher power—the inclination to act on such knowledge—could actually lead to a change in his smoking habits.

For the theologian, the higher nature principally refers to the new life of grace. The *habitus* of this higher nature consist in the infused moral virtues and, above all, the theological virtues of faith, hope, and charity. These enable the believer, faced with an habituation to some harmful practice or, for that matter, with any moral disorder, to perfect the relevant moral virtues through the agency of Christian faith and spiritual exercise. In the example cited, the smoker may come to recognize that the sacrifice of the pleasure which comes from smoking counts as part of the virtue of penitence and, therefore, to discover the required resolve to quit smoking in the example of Christ or the saints.

Aquinas stresses that human virtue, which makes a person tend to act in accordance with human nature, should be distinguished from divine or heroic virtue, which makes the same person act in accordance with some superior nature.[10] This distinction enables theological ethics to acknowledge the fact that Christian growth ordinarily entails a gradual release from disordered *habitus* (generally considered to result from the effects of original sin in each member of the human species) and the progressive acquisition of well-ordered *habitus*.[11] Alasdair MacIntyre observes that Christian monastic communities historically contributed to the development and practice of virtue because their structure allowed for members to embrace a common purpose and shared views about the means to achieve it.[12] Moralists formerly took such "dogmatic" questions for granted, but the difficulties many people experience in living according to the virtues requires that today we emphasize the life of faith, hope, and charity lived in the Church of Christ.

The present discussion of the moral virtues includes specific reference to both the acquired and infused moral virtues. These latter exist only in synchronization with the theological virtues, especially charity. Although the virtues cannot be reduced simply to various forms of loving God, charity does remain, as a text attributed to St. Ambrose puts it, the mother of the virtues.[13] As a result, theologians arqued about the place that acquired moral virtue has in the Christian life. Certain authors considered the acquired virtues unnecessary philosophical talk about matters that have been entirely changed as a result of the Gospel.[14] Still others fear that two sets of virtues in the human subject, one caused through human effort and the other the effect of divine grace, effectively presuppose a "two-layered" person.[15] These objections do merit careful examination. However, the New Testament clearly envisions that a conflict between what belongs to the order of flesh and what belongs to the order of spirit establishes the context for explaining the uniqueness of the salvation won by the blood of Christ. St. Paul himself offers the best justification for the existence of both infused and acquired virtues when he describes the anguish of one caught between the inclinations of the old self and the recognition of the power Christ's grace offers to those who believe.[16]

As a way of establishing a proper order between the activities of both acquired and infused virtues, virtue-centered moral theology relates specific moral matters to the broader perspectives of Christian doctrine. Although other theoreticians undoubtedly seek such integration, theological ethics dependent on a divine command theory runs into difficulty in making its chief tenets cohere with the sum of Christian beliefs. Consider how little emphasis the casuists, who built their complicated systems upon the assumption that the whole moral life involved observance of divinely ordained precepts, gave to the role played even by the virtue of faith itself in vitalizing the moral life. The casuist authors generally ignored such essential truths for the Christian life as the indwelling of the blessed Trinity in the souls of the just; the believer's mystical incorporation into the Body of Christ; the Immaculate Conception of the Virgin

Mary; and the intercession of the saints. If such important doctrines for the moral life were noted at all, they, along with discussions of virtue itself, were relegated to the area of spiritual or ascetical theology. Although today some Catholic authors, influenced by the Protestant emphasis on Christ and the moral life, do mention the fact of the Incarnation as one of importance for moral theology, few have developed the full implications which the mystery of the blessed Trinity along with those of the economy of salvation hold for Christian moral development.

But Christian ethics cannot remain an isolated discipline, united to the other branches of theology only by the same departmental chairperson. Adequate instruction on how to live according to the new dispensation of Gospel grace requires more than a developed ability to apply sophisticated modes of moral argumentation. Nor is virtue a codeword for the observance of juridically framed directives on avoiding sin. For example, consider how the distinction between false locution and lying conditions moral reasoning to proceed along consequentialist lines. Should one speak the truth only in circumstances where truthtelling does not risk a serious harm to persons? The concrete case usually cited is: Must one reply truthfully to the unjust occupation force's inquiry about the whereabouts of an individual unjustly pursued?[17] Obviously, the issues raise a spectrum of diverse views on the function of absolute prohibitions in morals as well as on the use of the category of non-moral evil.[18] But the weighing of an action's consequences alone cannot resolve this moral dilemma. Furthermore, an authentic Christian response to the example cited must take into account the fortitude of Christ, the gift of the Holy Spirit called counsel, and the New Testament beatitude, "Blessed are they who are persecuted for righteousness' sake, for theirs is the kingdom of heaven" (Mt 5:10). In brief, moral argumentation limited only to rationalistic modes of ethical decision making fails to provide a satisfactory theological resolution for such "crunch" questions in Christian ethics.

But why is this the case? Realist moral theology holds that God's knowledge of reality, which ultimately accounts for why a thing is of a certain kind, extends as well to moral "natures." The divine mind itself establishes a "thing"—in this case, the moral action—as a specific kind of being. Accordingly, the origin of the moral law does not result from an exercise of the divine will, as certain theorists suggest, ordaining one thing to be commanded and another thing to be forbidden. Rather, morality finds its source in the divine intellect. As I have said, Aquinas referred to this function of God's creative power as the *lex aeterna*, or the Eternal Law.[19] Insistence on the place of the Eternal Law in human activity recalls the fact that the moral order, like the order of nature, remains God's creation. And moral theology has no alternative but to respect the givens of that moral order when it proposes norms for right conduct. This stance likewise gives full attention to what one author calls part of Aquinas's lost legacy: the relationship of God's practical knowledge to situated human freedom.[20]

Due consideration of the *lex aeterna* would contribute much towards easing the repeated controversies, especially since the Enlightenment, over the role that natural law plays in Christian morality. All in all, the place of natural law in Christian morality remains limited. Aquinas contents himself with but a single question on the subject of natural law in his *Summa theologiae*. There he defines it as the rational creature's participation in the Eternal Law. Although this definition interests the moral theologian, it does not entail the grossly exaggerated conclusions alleged by those who reject natural law as if it were the equivalent of a psychic or biological determinism.[21] Natural law establishes the grounds for an authentic deployment of human freedom, one which meshes with the *lex aeterna*. The controversy following the publication of *Humanae vitae*, for instance, exposed how far misunderstanding the function of natural law in moral argumentation had gone.[22]

Finally, the Christian theologian teaches that the Holy Spirit provides special helps to ensure that a virtue-centered morality accomplishes all that the New Testament requires of the believer. The true goal of human existence surpasses the means available to our unaided human powers, and not even the grace of the infused virtues suffices for all the needs of the Christian life. Thus, Christian moral theology teaches that God provides special divine interventions which each believer requires in order to attain Gospel beatitude. These gifts of the Holy Spirit, as they are traditionally called, constitute specific kinds of divine mediations designed to aid the moral virtues. According to Aquinas's phrase, the gifts are present in the life of the believer *in adjutorium virtutuum*—as coming to the help of the virtues. The question can be raised: If virtue represents a maximum perfection of human capacities, what grounds can be established for additional instruments of divine agency? The answer can only be found in the pages of the New Testament where Jesus repeatedly promises his disciples the abiding divine presence for the purpose of completing his mission. "These things I have spoken to you, while I am still with you. But the Counsellor, the Holy Spirit, whom the Father will send in my name, he will teach you all things, and bring to your remembrance all that I have said to you" (Jn 14: 25–26).

THE NATURE OF MORAL VIRTUE

Medieval theology placed a high premium on the theological axioms handed down from the patristic tradition.[23] It comes as no surprise, then, that St. Augustine provided the definition of virtue which became accepted in the schools from the beginning of the thirteenth century. The actual phrasing of the definition amounts to a collation of texts excerpted from several of St. Augstine's works. We find it, for example, in the *Commentary on the Sentences* of Peter of Poitiers: "Virtue is a good quality of mind by which one lives righteously, of which no one can make bad use, which God works in us without us."[24] Of course, the definition as it stands applies only to the infused virtues which result from the agency of divine grace. Nonetheless, theologians who recognized the role of the acquired virtues in Christian theology found the definition a workable one. Aquinas remarking on the phrase "which God works in us without us," wrote: "Were this phrase omitted the remainder of the definition will be common to all the virtues, whether acquired or infused."[25]

When it speaks about virtue as a "good quality of mind," the Augustinian definition suggests the concept of *habitus*. As a generic category for virtue, *habitus* describes both the acquired human virtues as well as the infused moral virtues. Since a *habitus* amounts to a real shaping of our character, virtue ensures that one actually does "live righteously." Recall that readiness, ease, and joy characterize any performance which results from a virtuous *habitus*. Likewise, the confident claim that a virtue constitutes something "of which no one makes bad use" rests upon the fact of the real transformation of our intellectual, volitional, and emotional powers which a *habitus* accomplishes.

Authentic virtue, then, does not merely amount to developing the proper techniques for behavior. Although at times Aristotle talks about virtue as if it only provided skills for right conduct,[26] Christian theology recognizes in virtue an essentially different reality. From a theological perspective, virtue resembles an art. It amounts to possessing a talent or genius for doing the good human action in the same way that a true artist possesses a creative spirit that defies description according to the conventional norms; that is, virtue realizes a deliberate and efficacious modification of a person's capacity for performing well. It consists both in qualifying a person for the business of being human and a Christian for the business of being a Christian. Virtues both human and divine provide the apprenticeship required for a life of human excellence and evangelical perfection. New Testament discussions of the effect which divine grace works in the human person influence the way theological ethics understands virtue. St. Paul taught that conversion to a life of faith meant that one became a wholly new being in Christ, "trying to capture the prize for which Christ Jesus captured me" (Phil 3:12). Accordingly, Christian virtue must reveal the new nature which faith promises to those who are united with Christ.[27]

Formed by this biblical teaching, the ancient baptismal rituals sought to express, by imagery and metaphors, the radical change that Christian faith brings about in both the person and the actions of the believer. The Greek Fathers understood the immersion into the baptismal pool as representing the spiritual death of the "old self"—St. Paul's expression for what is yet unredeemed in us.[28] In addition, the early Fathers accepted the clothing of the newly baptized with white garments and other ritual gifts, such as the anointing with oil and the handing over of a lit candle, as symbolizing the neophyte's new state or *habitus*. All this figuratively represents what the New Testament calls the state of "adoptive sonship."[29] Of course, the orthodox Fathers took pains clearly to affirm that such a transformation could only result from the power of the Holy Spirit freely bestowed on the one baptized. As a result, the patristic tradition generally stressed the specific relationship in the baptized between incorporation into Christ through baptismal renewal and the establishment of moral rectitude through virtuous activity.[30] The medieval theologians preserved this patristic intuition by speaking about virtue as a "quality of mind."

Nevertheless, even certain medieval traditions proposed to describe virtue extrinsically. For example, those who follow the school of Duns Scotus define virtue in terms of a predicamental relation.[31] They teach that any action enjoys the potential for qualifying as virtuous on the condition that it conforms to some accepted rule of conduct, for example, that of charity. This way of defining virtue appears reasonable enough, especially given the New Testament's insistence on the centrality of *agape*. But such a scheme fails to convey that each virtue really accomplishes a modification in the character of the one who possesses it. Following the "predicamental relation" account, the substance of virtue consists in a neutral psychological reality. According to this hypothesis, no psychological organization in the virtuous person actually accounts for why one acts in a certain way.[32] As a result, one can only ethically evaluate the disposition to act in a certain manner by reference to some extrinsic principle or norm. So virtue for Scotus remains a matter of advised volition, but not actual transformation. On the other hand, Aquinas recognizes that the virtuous *habitus* itself explains this or that quality of action. Consequently, the Thomist school can compare virtue to such good qualities of the body as health or beauty, even if, as the Aristotelian definition of *habitus* requires, virtue remains a principle of operation.[33]

The requirement that virtue account for what is best in human development also argues for an intrinsic notion of virtue. St. Augustine stressed that no one could doubt that virtue makes the soul superlatively good.[34] Moreover, Aristotle held "that every virtue causes its possessors to be in a good state and to perform their functions well."[35] In addition to restating the essential connection between a *habitus* and its possessor, such axioms point up the requirement imposed by the New Testament command which Jesus gives to his disciples. He asks them to be perfect as the Heavenly Father is perfect (cf. Mt 5:48). According to the beatitudes, New Testament existence remains a full and complete life, one which embraces the great commandments of love of God and neighbor in every aspect. New Testament morality could never permit, as the casuist tradition implicitly suggested, that in some cases a minimum suffices to fulfill love's demands.

Since the goal or end of Christian love finds expression in the great commandments of love for God and love for neighbor, no virtue exists in actions which are set against those goals. Philosophers should only define virtue as a good operative *habitus* by reference to what constitutes a concrete perfection for human nature,[36] rather than whatever action betrays a given set of formal characterisitcs.[37] Certainly the theologian must define virtue only by reference to what contributes to the perfection of the image of God in each individual. The task is not made easier by the fact that such perfection consists ultimately in beatific union with the blessed Trinity. Beatitude, like love itself, remains too comprehensive and transcendental—some might say elusive—a category to serve as the basis for differentiating virute. Even so, the theologian must discover a means for establishing the concrete goals of the Christian life. This requires agreement on the principal features of a Christian anthropology. The virtues enumerated by St. Augustine, Gregory the Great, and Aquinas point one in the right direction. In any event, agnosticism about what concretely establishes moral goodness can hold no place in Christian moral theology. Contemporary debate concerning the status of moral absolutes emphasizes the need for renewed clarity on this issue.[38]

The New Testament authors make no claim about providing a systematic ethics of virtue. Virtue appears only as examples of authentic Christian behavior, as in the Pauline letters, or as means of stressing essential constituents of the Gospel message, as when they describe Jesus' humility and obedience.[39] Hence, those theologians who argue that Christian theology should only speak about the virtues found in the Bible miss the point of the need for talk about basic goods for human perfection. Theological ethics must rely on philosophical wisdom in order to elaborate a plan of life which respects the demands of the New Testament as well as the exigencies of human culture. This represents the way St. Thomas approached his treatment of the virtues. Because he understood the analogical character of the infused moral virutes, Aquinas did not hesitate to set forth some fifty virtues in the course of organizing the *secunda pars*, and he recognized that these acquired virtues constitute the primary analogates for their graced equivalents, the infused virtues. Given that theology—"theo-logia"—signifies a speech about God, theologians have no alternative but to use human language when speaking about the life of grace. Yet, the doctrine of analogy reminds us that the reality of our participation in the divine life transcends the limits of both human experience and language.

VIRTUE AND HUMAN CAPACITIES

Among the more profound insights that Christian theology borrows from Aristotelian anthropology is the doctrine that the substance of the soul remains distinct, both conceptually and really, from the capacities or faculties of the soul. This distinction derives from more basic metaphysical convictions concerning being and action as applied to the structure of a created agent. Thus Aquinas could argue that operations belong to a being, in this case, the human person, in the same way that a substance possesses certain accidental modifications.[40] Virtue qualifies directly the capacities of the soul, not its substance, such that each capacity—intellect, will, and sense appetites—operates according to its maximum performance. Aquinas proposes three lines of argumentation in support of this thesis: First, since the very nature of virtue implies the perfection of a power, virtue remains in that which it perfects; secondly, virtue is defined as an operative *habitus*, but all operation springs from the soul through some capacity; finally, virtue disposes to what is best, but the best always means an end to be achieved, which is either a being's own activity or something attained through it.[41] To say that virtue modifies a person through the powers of the soul does not mean that it accomplishes only a limited good.

Critics sometimes complain that such a conception of the soul, known since the eighteenth century as "faculty psychology," results in a fragmented impression of the human person. Rational psychology's systematic distortion of the approved theory contributed to these misgivings. Cognitive psychologists argue that a faculty conception of the human psyche leads to a divisive view of how human agency works, as if different "things" were happening all at once, but in separate compartments of the spirit. On the contrary, Christian anthropology actually stresses the substantial unity of the human person when it designates the soul as the body's form. A central feature of realist virtue theory recognizes that certain virutes, although they do qualify their own proper capacity, also affect other faculties of the soul. "And thus one virtue," writes Aquinas, "can belong to several capacities, so that it is principally in one but flows out to others, or helps in the interaction of one power being set in motion by and receiving from another."[42] For example, the theological virtues, although they have their "seat," as it is called, in the rational powers of the soul, can and do affect the sense appetites.

The interaction of one power or capacity with another helps the Christian, who lives by faith, attain wholeness, even in activities which arise from the sense appetites. Take the case of the converted profligate, one habituated to some form of sexual immoderation who receives the grace of repentance. What effective means to maintain the virtue of chastity are restored to the soul as part of God's merciful forgiveness? The theological virtue of hope alone enables the person to trust in God's merciful aid and powerful forgiveness. But hope remains a virtue of the rational appetite, while chastity requires a qualification of the concupiscible appetite whence originates sexual desire. Thus, only infused temperance actually accounts for the attainment of virtuous moderation in matters of sexual gratification. But infused temperance depends upon an individual's direct relationship with God. Only hope, although principally a quality of the will, can render such a relationship actual in the believer, with the result that the theological virtue flows out, so to speak, into the sense appetites.

In effect, then, the virtues can enjoy a reciprocity among themselves, and the distinction between the substance of the soul and its powers allows for such mutual influence. As a result, Christian theology can describe the virtuous life as an organic moral harmony which results from the proper cooperation of our rational and appetitive powers. Perhaps the principal operation where the interdependence of the virtues contributes to the overall unity of the moral life involves the relationship of the intellectual virtue of prudence to the moral virtues. The unique role of prudence in a realist virtue-centered morality permits Aristotle's doctrine of practical reasoning its full measure of influence in Christian theology.

Intellectual Virtues

Realist moral theology rejects the materialist view that thought remains the phenomenal product of physical forces at work in the relationship between a self and the world. Instead it affirms, along with the Christian faith, both the spiritual character and the singular dignity of each human intellect. Although philosophers do dispute what constitutes the nature of the soul and its final destiny, theologians traditionally have recognized the connection between the doctrine of the immortality of the human soul and its immateriality.[43] Even given the spiritual character of the intellect, thinking, like the exercise of other human powers, requires virtue in order to operate well. Here good operation includes acquisition of the kinds of knowledge human intelligence has the capacity to develop. Intellectual virtue is required for the acquisition of any specific body of knowledge. Although theology speaks principally of the intellectual virtues of understanding, science, and wisdom, the classic definition of science remains broad enough to include all branches of human learning.

Important as the intellectual virtues remain for human life, they do not contribute directly to the constitution of moral character. The Christian imperative to love God and neighbor cannot be fulfilled by simply knowing how to act well. As countless situations demonstrate, people of learning, either for reasons of individual choice or on account of moral weakness, do not use their knowledge in order to develop virute in their lives. Because they do not ensure that "no one can make bad use of them," as the definition of a moral virtue requires, the scholastics referred to the intellectual virtues as virtues after a fashion (*secundum quid*). Indeed, one without the appropriate moral virtue can use an intellectual virtue to promote evil ends. This happens, for instance, when instruments of technological warfare fall into the hands of persons who do not respect the virtues of justice within the human community or when a financier uses professional confidences in order to facilitate the unjust acquisition of corporate funds.

When the virtues of the intellect properly interact with the moral virtues, the former take on a new importance in the moral life. Prudence and faith (both virtues which have their seat in the intellect) interact with other virtues inasmuch as they give intelligent direction to the moral and theological life. The infused virtue of prudence amounts to more than just a technique for acting well; rather, it embodies a real participation in the wisdom of Christ, which, as the Gospel makes clear, belongs in a special way to little children. Christian theology contributes to a softening of the hard distinctions that classical philosophy established between the two classes of virtues. Moreover, the specifically New Testament virtue of humility guards against all intellectual pretension to equate knowledge with moral excellence.

VIRTUES OF THE RATIONAL APPETITE

The impact of the will on the whole of Christian life, especially the ordering of the human person towards God, remains a controverted topic in other areas of theology. Certain authors claim that the will by its very nature enjoys a kind of determination towards the ultimate good of human well-being. Among them are those theologians who affirm that the very relationship to God himself finds a transcendental foundation in the structure of human willing. The view that the will's natural inclination alone suffices to account for the development of a complete moral life suggests the position of Romantic philosophers who speculated about the shape unadorned human nature might take in a world where civilization, including moral culture, had not begun to spoil the pristine nobility of the race. Although Christian theology accepts the doctrine of a natural appetite for good as a constitutive part of its anthropology, the Romantic view goes considerably beyond what a correct reading of the tradition allows, especially when one gives due attention to the effects of original sin. And those moralists who stress the fundamental goodness of human nature, thereby making it almost impossible for moral evil to occur, certainly seem to ignore a necessary distinction required for any intelligent discussion of this question. Moral realists, on the contrary, emphasize the distinction between the structure of the human will and the individual willing. Why? Because they realize that, although the human will in principle remains naturally inclined towards its proper object, that is, the good of the one willing and a life according to reason, the individual willing, for a variety of reasons, may not be "naturally" thus inclined. Experience offers the best proof that this distinction exists in reality, and not simply in the minds of some moralists.

Accordingly, a given will, like other human powers, requires its own virtues in order to act towards the perfection of human life. These virtues, justice, hope, and charity, play an essential part in the virtuous formation of the whole person. Of course, to specify distinct virtues for the will runs counter to the argument of some theorists who maintain that the essential requirement for Christian life involves a generic act of the will, a basic option, as it were, to live a life directed towards God. "The term 'fundamental option'," writes one contemporary moralist, "means the stable orientation or life direction that exists at the core level of the human person."[44] Critics of this fundamental option approach note that something so general as an orientation at the core level of the human person cannot possibly ensure virtuous activity in the highly complex matters that make up the moral life. Rather, the ability to act properly at the "categorical" level, as theoreticians of the fundamental option refer to the world of particular moral choices, requires the distinctive formation that virtue gives to human powers in order that they achieve their ends. In the case of the will, choosing a particular good action requires justice and charity, the virtues which reside in the will. Nor should the function of these virtues be confused with the role of charity as the form of all the Christian virtues. For in addition to animating the whole theological life, charity also regulates human loving with respect to its own proper objectives.[45]

Nonetheless, the will as a faculty does operate according to its own dynamic and does function differently from the way the intellect does. Specifically, the intellect requires a basic *habitus* of first principles, the virtue of understanding, in order even to initiate its activity. The will, on the other hand, possesses an out-going, tendential structure and therefore requires no special *habitus* in order to move towards its object, the good. Indeed, were the supreme

Good to become present to the human person, the human will would choose God immediately. We would act without hesitation. Of course, in this life the beatifying presence of God does not appear. Rather, divine grace allows the believer to choose God gradually over the course of a lifetime, provided that one continue to live by faith. Hence the life of Christian faith both requires and ensures that virtue shape the will, along with the other powers, in order to integrate the great variety of human goods into the perfection of choosing and loving God. Thus the virtue of justice conforms the person to created ends which surpass self-interest and establish the common good. Theological charity enables the Christian to embrace the goodness of God and to love self and neighbor in accord with this goodness and under the impulse of the Holy Spirit.

VIRTUES OF THE SENSE APPETITES

The question of how much rational control can effectively shape emotional behavior remains one of the most disputed elements in both philosophical and clinical psychology.[46] Although most Christian thinkers share the view that our rational powers can exercise some form of control over the lower powers of sense and emotion, they do not always agree on how this dynamic works. A strong tradition within Christian spirituality, usually associated with St. Bonaventure and others of his school, denies that the sense powers as such are capable of possessing authentic virtue.[47] At best, reason can exercise a kind of despotic control over human emotion. Reason acts like a tyrant enforcing some rule upon unwilling citizens. The view that original sin substantially amounts to unregulated concupiscence provides, at least historically, some explanation of why certain authors found it difficult to locate divinely given virtue in the concupiscible appetite. In addition, a generic kind of Platonism favored the view that human rational powers could alone exercise the kind of firm control required to regulate the erratic impulses of the sense appetites. Insofar as this view has been accepted as authentic Christian teaching on the matter of reason's control over emotion, humanists have understandably regarded the Christian outlook on this point with suspicion.[48]

A realist view, such as proposed by Aquinas and others, holds a different opinion on this crucial matter of maintaining emotional stability. Aquinas introduced an important distinction into the discussion when he argued that the irascible and concupiscible powers can be considered in two ways: First, in themselves, as they form part of the sensitive appetites; and, secondly, as they share in the life of reason, which in the human person is what the emotions are meant to do. In this latter sense, he concluded, "the irascible or the concupiscible power can be the seat of human virtue, for in so far as each participates in reason, it is a principle of a human act."[49] Admittedly, the virtuous development of the sense appetites does require a definite relationship to right reason, but Aquinas and those who follow him insist that the sensible powers themselves do possess the capacity for authentic virtuous formation. These powers constitute true "seats" for virtue. A Christian reading of Aristotle supplies much of the anthropological warrant for making this assertion about the sense appetites.[50]

A text from Aquinas provides a clear explanation of this important point for Christian moral theology.

> The body is ruled by the soul, and the irascible and concupiscible powers by reason, but in different ways. The body blindly obeys without contradiction where it is born to be moved by the soul. Hence Aristotle says that 'the soul rules the body with a despotic rule,' as a master rules his slave: here the body's entire movement is attributed to the soul. For this reason virtue is not in the body but in the soul. The irascible and concupiscible powers, however, have no such blind response. Instead, they have their own proper movement, by

which, at times, they go against reason; hence Aristotle says that reason rules the irascible and concupiscible powers with political control, as free men are ruled who have in some matters a will of their own. This is why virtues are required in these powers, so that they may be well fitted for operation.[51]

In effect, a realist moral theology seeks to enunciate a sound psychological basis for its claim that virtue can radically transform human behavior of every sort.

Moral realism unequivocally rejects all forms of anthropological dualism. Christian life does not simply embody a spiritual ideal. Rather, the concupiscible and irascible sense appetites, which, in themselves comprise the emotional life of the human person, possess the capacity for true virtuous formation ordered to the authentic finalities of both nature and grace. One author summarizes the significance of this doctrine in this way. "Amid the exuberance and the dejection, the foolhardiness and the fear of anyone's emotions, moderation, stability and rectitude are possible. The rule of reason does not refuse to recognize the good within the object of the appetites, but it is aware that a particular good is to be loved as such. At the time, in the place, and in the way the limitations of the sense objects allow, the appetites may give themselves to their proper objects."[52]

Otherwise, the "baptized" Stoic view that Christianity demands highly motivated will power for the fulfillment of its moral requirements offers a much less convincing approach. Although St. Bonaventure taught that the virtues of temperance and fortitude literally reside in the will, the exercise of despotic control by the will over unruly passions can only fail to accomplish its purpose. Indeed, such an exercise of the will too closely resembles the process of repression wherein, even though the ideational representation of some object of desire is withheld from consciousness, the object is no less an object of desire for that reason. Furthermore, experience amply shows that when the will fails in its struggle with the passions, it tends to withdraw from the conflict. By rejecting all attempts to modify the emotional life by means other than authentic virtue formation, moral realism offers a more optimistic proposal for living a holy life.[53]

Discussion of the way virtue affects our emotional life leads to questions of utmost importance for theological ethics. Current dissatisfaction with certain elements of Christian morality centers almost exclusively on the virtues of the concupiscible appetites. Those who advocate changes, for example, in the way the Church explains the requirements of Christian sexual morality undoubtedly do so, at least in part, because of the overwhelming resistance which modern culture, to define the factor broadly, puts up against the practice of purity and chastity. This sociological datum merits some attention. However, in addition to pointing out the obstacles to a virtuous life in the twentieth century, theologians should also accept the responsibility of explaining how the believer can fulfill the demands of virtue enunciated by Church teaching. Otherwise, instead of a Christ who transforms culture, we proclaim that our culture conquers Christ. In the work of evangelization, there exists no room for compromise on what the grace of Christ can accomplish in anyone, no matter what his or her state or condition may be.

CHRISTIAN FAITH AND DISORDERED EMOTIONS

Since there exists so much misunderstanding about the relationship of the will to the sense appetites, a closer study of one of Aquinas's texts affords us a chance to examine this important question for the Christian life. St. Thomas enunciates a psychological principle upon which a great deal of Christian moral theology depends. In *Summa theologiae* Ia q. 80, he poses the question of whether sensitive appetite and rational or intellectual appetite are distinct capacities. He began to lay out the specific features of his doctrine on the powers or capacities of the soul in q. 77, which contains the important teaching on the distinction between the substance of the soul and its powers. Then in q. 78, he describes the vegetative powers (nutrition, growth, and generation) and the sensitive powers (the five external senses and the four internal senses: memory, imagination, the *sensus communis* or common sense, and the *vis cogitativa* or cognitive power) of the soul. Next he considers the general features of the intellect in q. 79. The appetitive powers of the soul occupy the remaining questions of the tract on the psychological structure of the human person. Because of the importance this anthropological postulate holds for the practical living out of the Christian moral life, we will focus on the distinction Aquinas draws between the sense appetites and the intellectual appetite. This distinction particularly illumines the relationship of theological hope to the moral virtues, especially those *circa passiones*, those which shape human emotional life.

The arguments against the thesis of q. 80, a. 2 propose reasons for thinking that appetite remains undifferentiated in the individual human. Or, to put it another way, no difference exists between what sense perception produces in human appetite—the movement of desire—and what an individual could really be said to rationally "will" or want. In reply, Aquinas cites the opinion of Aristotle in the *De Anima*. There the Philosopher not only distinguishes the two powers of appetite but also asserts that the higher power, the rational appetite, can control the lower appetite. Admittedly, this simply assertion requires considerable nuance, especially since many people experience great difficulty when it comes to controlling the urges of sense. Aristotle was content to describe what happened in the best of individuals; he was under no constraint to take into account the difference that a universal call to holiness would make for ethics. Or, to look at matters from a different perspective, the ultimate truth of Aristotle's intuition about how human nature should function could only be realized as a result of the New Law of grace, because only grace restores that integrity to human nature which makes living a fully rectified life possible.

Aquinas begins his reply by citing the fundamental Aristotelian doctrine that the appetitive "is born to be moved as a result of apprehension."[54] Now the objects of appetite, whether nourishment, sexual gratification, a standard of living, the help of the saints, or union with God, themselves possess the ability to move the powers of appetite. Yet, each of these objects remains unaffected by the fact that it is desired. In this regard, God and an apple are the same; neither changes as a result of eliciting desire in a created power. On the other hand, the appetite does effect a change in the person who becomes drawn towards a particular thing. In the large sense of the term, this is the movement of love. By their nature, the appetitive powers seek to possess the object of attraction as the ultimate term of love.

Since there exist two different classes of objects which exercise an attractive pull on the human person, two distinct appetites need to be distinguished. Just as the sensitive appetites can only interact with sense objects, so intellectual objects (such as seeking the common good, pursuing a life of study, loving God) require a suitable appetite which fits them. Although the sense appetite can be moved to flee a life-threatening danger, for example, from the heat of a burning building, only the rational appetite can discriminate as to how to flee virtuously (or, in some circumstances, actually to choose to withstand such a threat, perhaps in an attempt to save another person). To take another example, the sense appetite can be drawn by an object which may involve sexual gratification, such as happens in extra-marital coitus, but only the rational appetite can discern the moral truth that a virtuous love of friendship excludes this form of carnal communication. As Aquinas points out, there exists an essential difference between what the intellectual appetite wills and what the sense appetites want. Thus, nothing prohibits the believer from exercising an act of authentic personal choosing, for example, to will the good of virtue, even in the presence of strong sense desire for some object opposed to it. Spiritual writers underscore the importance of this truth when they encourage believers to face temptations against the moral virtues by recourse to acts of faith, hope, and charity.

Sense desire remains indiscriminate, with the result that it cannot really choose. Why? Because nothing in the structure of either the irascible or concupiscible appetites allows them to discriminate a good-to-be-sought or an evil-to-be-avoided. Only the intellectual virtue of prudence can discern the good-as-meant, namely, how this good or evil should be virtuously embraced or avoided under a particular set of concrete circumstances. Aquinas stresses how the "intellect penetrates the will with its act and object the way it does any other particular objects of understanding, like stone or wood, which all fall within the field of being and truth."[55] It belongs to the intellect, then, not only to discriminate moral truths, for example, flesh to be cherished from flesh which is abused, but also to embrace the truths of faith. The theological virtue of faith, then, unites the believer to everything which God discloses about Christian life. In short, there exist no purely speculative truths of revelation. Every truth—for instance, that God loves us because he is good, not because we are; that Jesus saves us by his death; that Mary is immaculately conceived; that the sacraments are efficacious for our salvation—contributes to the perfection of the moral life.

Thus, even when the emotions are disturbed, the Christian believer can still rationally choose the truth of God's goodness, the power of the blood of Christ, the maternal mediation of the blessed Virgin Mary, the efficacy of the sacraments—in short, the whole economy of salvation—because faith penetrates the rational appetite with these good things. For although the virtue of faith is in the intellect, it nonetheless motivates the virtue of hope whereby the believer clings to God's omnipotent mercy as the source of salvation. This spiritual clinging forms the basis for the whole moral life and surely fulfills the meaning of the many places in the New Testament, especially in the Johannine writings, where Jesus encourages his disciples to stay closely united with him and his Heavenly Father. "He who abides in me, and I in him, he it is that bears much fruit, for apart from me you can do nothing" (Jn 15:5). Theological hope especially draws the Christian, who recognizes his or her moral feebleness, to cleave to God's mercy and power.

Furthermore, the believer can make this efficacious choice for salvation through the agency of the rational appetite, even in the face of a whole range of disordered sense-urges. Living according to this faith conviction first requires being instructed in how to make an act of faith, which in turn requires being practically convinced that God loves you because he is good and not because you are. Otherwise, at this point, people would simply give up in despair, because they would falsely conclude that even if salvation is promised, it is not possible for one tempted in this or that way. Such a Pelagian understanding of the Christian moral life reveals an even more pernicious premise, namely, that one need achieve a certain state of holiness before meriting God's love. With this mentality, no one would achieve holiness, since each individual would always seek to make the initial break with sin without the benefit of recourse to divine grace. Still, how many people, desirous of loving God, are nonetheless blackmailed by this quite false understanding of how God's love works? But the authentic teaching on the matter remains clear. St. Ambrose, commenting on the verse of the Canticle, "Hark! my beloved is knocking," wrote: "When does God the Word most often knock at your door? . . . He visits in love those in trouble and temptation, to save them from being overwhelmed by their trials. His head is covered with dew or moisture when those who are his body are in distress."[56]

Existentially, then, this doctrine of the distinction between the two kinds of appetite serves an extremely important function in an appropriate theology of the Christian life and spirituality. It allows the theologian to affirm, in a practical way, the ultimate triumph of God's power over fallen nature. Later in his discussion of the human person, Aquinas asks whether the irascible and concupiscible appetites obey reason. He concludes that the sense appetites obey reasoned discourse for two reasons. First, because particular truths can both calm wrath and fear or arouse them. And, secondly, since human action requires the "consensus" of the higher appetite, the unity of the human person requires that the sense appetites obey the rational appetite. The teaching could appear to have little significance for Christian life, and even to be naive, were it not understood that, for the believer, the "particular" truths which control the appetites are the very truths of our salvation. These derive from the person and teaching of Jesus Christ, who alone sets forth the whole economy of salvation. If one considers the perfection of human life, the desired "consensus" of the will for choosing moral good in every sitaution can only come from divine grace, no matter what the state of the emotions may be at any given time. This gift of grace belongs to God's adopted sons and daughters only as a result of the personal union they enjoy with Christ, the Son by nature, in the Church of faith and sacraments. "Blessed then is the one," concludes St. Ambrose, "at whose door Christ stands and knocks. Our door is faith; if it is strong enough, the whole house is safe."[57]

4. PRUDENCE AND THE MORAL VIRTUES

COMMUNIO AND THE MORAL LIFE

Christian revelation unequivocally teaches that the redemption won by Christ results in the establishment of a new social order that is achieved by means of a transformation in each individual person. The book of Revelation presents the vision of a great multitude: "Who are these, clothed in white robes, and whence have they come? These are they who have come out of the great tribulation; they have washed their robes and made them white in the blood of the Lamb" (Rev 7:9–14). St. Paul, in an effort to explicate the "great tribulation," describes the personal conflict which those who are transformed in the blood of Christ escape: "I do not understand my own actions. For I do not do what I want, but I do the very thing I hate" (Rom 7:15). Authentic Christian salvation constitutes both a liberation from the contradiction of sin and the restoration of the rectitude of grace. The First Letter of Peter reminds its readers: "As obedient children, do not be conformed to the passions of your former ignorance, but as he who called you is holy, be holy yourselves in all your conduct" (1 Pet 1:13–14).

The full experience of Christian community requires that each member of the Church break away from patterns of sinful behavior. By definition, as the Old Testament stories about the effects of Adam's sin remind us, sin divides.

72

Charity unites. But since the human race was restored to charity through the sacrificial death of the Son of God, the theological life necessarily entails a participation in the cross of Christ. The Christian life does not develop in anyone without personal sacrifice and the undertaking of satisfactory works. St. Paul frequently refers to this sacrificial element in Christian life, particularly when he speaks about virtues and vices.

> Now the works of the flesh are plain: fornication, impurity, licentiousness, idolatry, sorcery, enmity, strife, jealousy, anger, selfishness, dissension, party spirit, envy, drunkenness, carousing and the like. I warn you, as I warned you before, that those who do such things shall not inherit the kingdom of God. But the fruit of the Spirit is love, joy, peace, patience, kindness, goodness, self-control; against such there is no law. And those who belong to Christ Jesus have crucified the flesh with its passions and desires (Gal 5:19–24).

In a phrase, Christian conversion always remains ordered to the development of the virtuous life.

The transformation of our moral lives effected by renewal in Christ occurs within the community of the Church. This happens principally through the sacramental actions established by the New Law, but also through the exercise of Christian charity, that is, when the members of the Church love one another properly. The eucharist, the principal sacrament of the Church, especially points out the relationship between sacramental efficacy and the realization of Christian *communio*.[1] Nevertheless, a full and adequate explanation of what constitutes the evangelical life requires more than the instruction provided by the New Testament for worship. The Christian moral theologian takes on an even more formidable task than that of the liturgist or sacramental theologian. Moral theology concerns every human action. As a result, the moral theologian assumes responsibility for showing how the once and for all character of Christian redemption, as the Letter to the

Hebrews explains it,[2] means that whatever the grace of Christ touches in human existence becomes radically new and different.

Within the Church, emphases in ascetical theology vary from one century to another; the contemporary mood looks more to the glorious wounds of the Savior than to the suffering which made them so. One point, however, always requires specific consideration, namely, the death of the "old self" does not constitute a complete destruction of the human powers and capacities given in nature. Rather, the process of image-restoration reshapes the activity of those powers and capacities towards authentic virtue. At times, certain ascetical theologicans, especially those influenced by seventeenth-century French piety, forgot this basic and important truth of catholic spirituality. As a result, they stressed a strained discontinuity between Christian practice and everyday human life. Such a position, since it frowns on even ordinary pleasures such as music, drink, and dance, remains foreign to the orthodox theological tradition.[3] In moral theology, this unwholesome dualism sometimes expresses itself in odd ways, as when the French Jesuit Jean Surin writes to one of his *pénitentes*: "Your sins can't sully God, because sin and God abide in different places: Sin tarries in your nature and God in your spirit."[4]

Christian spirituality, however, does not permit such a cleavage of body and soul. Though one might adduce other reasons to support this thesis, authentic freedom requires a unified conception both of the human person and of the virtuous life. After all, St. Augustine formulated the axiom that God who created the human race without assistance, would not redeem the race without its cooperation.[5] Or, to put the truth in more personalist terms, "Are you not yet attracted?" he wrote, "Pray that you may be attracted."[6] The Christian tradition, as several significant controversies clearly indicate, has unwaveringly insisted upon the place that freedom holds in the moral life both of the individual and of the community.[7]

Yet diverse trends in philosophy and, recently, various schools of psychology offer competing explanations about the very nature of human freedom. Since the question of the priority of divine grace in human initiative especially provokes serious misunderstandings, one specific point deserves particular mention: Does a virtue-centered moral theology fail to emphasize the importance of divine grace in the practice of the Christian life? Because they reply affirmatively to this question, many people back away from considering the Christian life in terms of an exhaustive list of virtues on the grounds that doing so puts the burdensome character of the old dispensation into the New Law of grace.[8] The virtues appear to constrain the exercise of liberty promised to the members of Christ's Body. It is important to recall that authentic Catholic teaching on the life of divine grace asserts that the created will possesses no power to work unto salvation apart from a prior, free exercise of the divine initiative. The scholastics called this a *gratia operans*. The infused virtues, at least in their initial formation, result from the freely bestowed grace of the Holy Spirit active in the lives of believers, and not from a sheer exercise of will power.

In like manner, the enduring human ability to live the virtuous life always requires the continued presence of divine cooperative grace.[9] "The activity of the Holy Spirit," writes Aquinas, "by which he moves and protects us is not confined to the effect of the habitual gift which he causes in us; but besides this effect he, together with the Father and the Son, moves and protects us."[10] This emphasis on freely given grace points to the central place which the person of Jesus Christ holds in a virtue-centered moral theology and in the achievement of authentic human freedom. According to the classical thesis on the threefold grace of the Incarnate Son, the humanity of Christ alone serves as the instrument of divine life for each member of the

Church. Christ fulfills this function by exercise of what is known as his "capital" grace, or the grace of headship. In turn, the possession of such grace means that the believer, inasmuch as he or she remains united with Christ, enjoys the radical ability to develop freely and to live fully all of the virtues.[11] In his catechetical instruction on the creed, St. Cyril of Jerusalem explains that the Church is called catholic "because it heals and cures unrestrictedly every type of sin that can be committed in soul or in body, and because it possesses within itself every kind of virtue that can be named, whether exercised in actions or in words or in some kind of spiritual charism."[12]

PRUDENCE AND THE MORAL VIRTUES

When contemporary students of moral theology talk about Christian freedom, they expect that the discussion will also address personal responsibility. For example, Charles Curran emphasizes responsibility as a principal consideration in moral decision making.[13] Debate in theological ethics about what constitutes a responsible Christian, however, frequently ignores the role that the intellectual virtues play in achieving this stage of maturity. As a result, fewer theologians emphasize the position of Christian wisdom in the structure and development of moral responsibility.[14] Despite this lack of emphasis, the intellectual virtues do occupy an indispensable place in the mature Christian life and their function surpasses the mere informing of conscience.

The relationship between the intellectual and moral virtues principally involves one virtue of the practical intellect, the cardinal virtue of prudence. The role of prudence in Christian morals reflects the importance which the New Testament and the tradition which follows it assign to divine wisdom in the life of the believer.[15] This tradition differs from the Kantian and post-Kantian views on the role of 'pure reason' in moral theory. These positions generally affirm that the categories of practical reason intervene at each discreet moment of moral choice, but their normative character derives from sources which remain *a priori* and, therefore, independent of cumulative human experience and inclinations. Christian wisdom, on the other hand, develops in an individual, at least in part, as a result of both inclination and experience. Thus, Aquinas insists that the moral virtues and prudence operate according to a kind of synergy, that is, they exercise a causal influence on each other. As a result of this synergy of prudence and the virtues, Christian wisdom, in accord with *lex aeterna*, really enters into and shapes the appetitive life of the individual. In turn, the rectified appetitive powers enable prudence to grasp intellectually the will's bent towards the good. As J. O. Urmson observes, "How different this is from Kant's view that an action in accordance with one's inclination, *Neigung*, has no moral worth!"[16]

Virtuous activity means human activity at its best. "Every virtue," wrote Aristotle, "causes its possessors to be in good state and to perform their functions well."[17] Virtue requires that the whole person participate in the perfection of virtue. There exists a difference between actions which arise out of authentic virtue and those which result when a person exercises self-control at a particular moment. For example, on occasion an individual who lacks the right conformity which temperance establishes in the concupiscible appetite can actually choose to perform a particular temperate act. In order to distinguish this kind of action from that of authentic virtue, theologians refer to such discreet acts as the result of certain dispositions. For example, the decision to act temperately in a given situation produces a continent action, that is, a simple exercise of self-control. Or, when it is the case of simply commanding the irascible appetites to act or to refrain from action, the individual shows a disposition towards perseverance. In both cases, the actions unquestionably do not represent authentic virtue, nor do they require prudence.

As we have already observed, virtue imples more than the will to commit a virtuous action. Authentic virtue exists only when the human person possesses a certain interior conformity of both the cognitive and the appetitive powers to the purposes or goals of a virtuous life. The medieval theologians referred to these purposes as "ends." Consequently, to take a familiar example, in order for a husband and wife to fulfill virtuously the purpose or end of conjugal chastity, their embrace of married love must amount to more than the simple act of coitus. Although continent spouses could fulfill the marriage obligation in precisely that way, genuinely virtuous wedlock means more than a shared bed. The partners in a Christian marriage should love one another as a result of an authentic conformity to all that the married state encompasses as its purpose or end, including mutual love for each other.[18] Once this virtuous conformity takes root in the married couple, conjugal chastity no longer remains a matter of simply performing the marriage act or, for that matter, refraining from it. Rather, virtue now makes the manifold expressions of married love and communication easy, prompt, and joyful within the context of a complete and satisfactory married life.

The development of this conformity to the ends or purposes of the moral virtues does not happen accidentally. The principal means for such a development remains the moral virtue of prudence. Although prudence perfects our *intellectual* powers, moralists traditionally include it among the four cardinal *moral* virtues. St. Augustine wrote that prudence is love choosing wisely between the helpful and the harmful.[19] But Aquinas, recognizing the importance of the Aristotelian doctrine on practical reasoning, qualified this definition of prudence. "The initial activity of the appetitive power is loving," he wrote, "and it is in this sence that prudence is said to be love, not that of its nature it is a kind of love, but because its activity is caused by love."[20]

THE ROLE OF PRUDENCE

The moral virtue of prudence plays an essential role in the Christian moral life. Historically, the excessive preoccupation of the casuists with the formation and states of conscience reduced prudence to a subsidiary place in Christian moral theory. They treated prudence as the equivalent of discretion or caution, as if only certain people needed to practice it under specific circumstances. Popular usage, moreover, confirmed this erroneous impression. The current renewal of moral theology affords the opportunity for retrieving a correct understanding of this cardinal virtue in moral decision making.

Realist moral theology assigns prudence a large and ambitious role for prudence must assure that each human action embody both the complete form of moral goodness and, at the same time, the truth claims of moral science. Christian prudence, then, combines both the intellectual emphasis of classical philosophy, for example, Aristotle's doctrine of *phronesis*, with the quest of the Christian tradition—"*amor meus, pondus meum*," my love, my inclination. Each of these features of prudence reveal distinctive elements of New Law morality. Aquinas, especially, recognized this fact when he inquired about the burdensomeness of the New Law. Observing that the New Law prohibited certain interior mental acts not expressly prohibited in all cases in the Old Law, he wrote:

> But this is extremely difficult for someone without the virtue; as Aristotle himself says, it is easy to do what the just man does, but to do it in the way in which the just man does it, that is, with pleasure and promptly, is difficult for someone who does not have the virtue of justice. The same point is

made in I John, that "his commandments are not burdensome," on which Augustine comments that "they are not burdensome to someone who loves, but they are burdensome to
someone who does not love."[21]

Prudence, then, transforms knowledge of moral truth into
specific virtuous actions which are not burdensome, that
is, which do not include friction, internal strife, forcing
oneself.[22]

Generally speaking, the developed virtue of prudence
represents the achievement of a complete moral culture in
the human person whose intelligence and appetites function harmoniously towards good human activity. Likewise
imprudence, the vice opposed to prudence, results from the
influence of disordered passions or vicious habits as well
as from some deficiency in moral learning. First, prudence
shapes the discursive development of practical reason towards the making of a moral judgment. Although prudence
is a virtue of the mind, it nonetheless ensures conformity
between the several stages of moral knowledge and the
appetite's bent towards good ends, especially, the basic
goods of human fulfillment. Secondly, prudence is imperative. It regulates the finalization of a moral action insofar
as its principal act, command, terminates in the enjoyment
of human flourishing. To sum up, to imperate a virtuous
action remains an act of the intellect, but, in order to effect
this, prudence requires that the commanded action conform to the inclinations of rectified appetites.

One may easily distinguish this meaning of prudence
from the intellectualist conception of the virtue, such as
proposed by Duns Scotus. In an opinion similar to that of
Kant, Scotus alleged that prudence remains a kind of pure
knowing. Though he held that the virtue perfects human
intelligence, Scotus also averred that prudence can operate
independent of the influence of right appetite.[23] According
to this conception, prudence, defined as a simple intellectual virtue, can provide direction for the moral life, but it

can contribute nothing towards shaping the appetites to follow that direction.[24] Contemporary controversies about the purpose and role of conscience indicate the perennial allure this kind of proposal holds in theological ethics. Such a construal of how virtue operates effectively eliminates what we will describe as the "unitive function" of prudence in the moral life. Any theory which supposes that the actual shape of one's appetites does not affect the principal cognitive moral faculty—whether it be called conscience or not—advances an asymmetric view of the moral life.

The truth of this assertion may be seen if one considers the potential for inevitable conflicts between what conscience dictates and what appetite inclines or strives for. Given a sovereign view of conscience, only two alternatives are possible. On the one hand, conscience can assume the role of a dictator and judge, employing psychological guilt as the principal instrument for enforcing its commands. Or, on the other hand, conscience, especially when confronted with strong but disordered appetite, can issue an exemption from the observance of any moral norm which otherwise would conflict with the untoward craving of appetite. To implement the second alternative supposes a kind of autonomy alien to New Testament liberty. Since the first alternative can result in much psychic and spiritual distress, the option for "freedom" through exemption naturally holds a much broader appeal. Not a few contemporary moral theologians stand ready to allow a complete range of erratic behavior, especially in the area of sexual morality, on the basis that strong, felt dispositions justify conscientious exceptions in a given case or in an entire class of cases.[25] To put it differently, whenever conscience plays an autonomous role in the moral life, even with due insistence on the obligation to inform it, the importance of a rational measure harmoniously directing and shaping the movement of appetite towards the authentic ends of human nature vanishes.

For the most part, modern moral philosophy chooses disjunctively between emotion or reason as the principal justification for moral norms.[26] Neither of these partial methods, however, can affirm the synergy between intellect and appetite in the way realist moral theology describes the working of the virtue of prudence. First, rational principles, no matter how well worked out, can only partially assure that a particular human action actually instantiates a full measure of moral goodness. Secondly, human appetites lack in themselves the ability to develop a correct moral measure, even if, as Aquinas claims,[27] they contain the seeds of virtue. Only the virtue of prudence shapes practical reason in accordance with authentic moral knowledge and, therefore, renders it capable of conforming human behavior towards the achievement of virtuous ends already in a sense possessed by rectified appetites.[28]

THE UNITIVE FUNCTION OF PRUDENCE

Drawing on a tradition first formulated by the classical philosopher Boethius, Christian theology generally understands the human person, at least materially, as "the individual substance of a rational nature."[29] On the assumption that no contingent being can offer an adequate explanation for its own existence, human nature requires God both for its coming-to-be and its preservation in being. As a result of the relationship which exists between God and the rational creature, each human person possesses natural law inclinations and receives moral instruction. Aquinas defines the natural law as the participation of the rational creature in the Eternal Law.[30] Recall that the Eternal Law is nothing else than God's wise plan for directing every movement and action in creation.

Creation in the image of God means that the moral life derives from the *lex aeterna*, which Trinitarian theology usually attributes to the *Logos*, the eternal Son. All that God communicates to us by way of instruction, broadly

construed, includes whatever moral reason alone can discover along with the entirety of moral truth revealed in
Christ. Although some authors question this thesis, it is a
reasonable assumption that the teaching of all moral truth,
including the principles of natural law, fulfills an essential
part of the Church's prophetic role.[31] Christian moral
teaching remains a faith-knowledge even when certain elements of the teaching, for example, the common precepts
of the natural law, do not necessarily require faith for their
full comprehension. Aquinas suggested that moral precepts
fall into three categories: the most general precepts of the
natural law; natural law precepts which require an eluci-
dation by those advanced in moral wisdom; and precepts
revealed by God.[32]

In using *imago Dei* as a theological category to describe
human nature, theologians consciously make a statement
about the origins and the destiny of the human person. In
order to discover where the created representation of the
blessed Trinity principally manifests itself in us, St. Augustine pointed theology towards the chief psychological activities in human nature. Hence, knowing and loving serve as
the focal points both for the doctrine of the *imago Dei* and
for natural law theory. The *imago*, at least aptitudinally,
images the blessed Trinity when, in accord with natural
law inclinations, it performs the basic operations of the
cognitive and appetitive capacities. In particular, this image
of representation, as the scholastics called it, seeks perfection: first, in loving certain ends but, especially, in conforming to the Supreme Good; secondly, in knowing certain truths but, especially, in adhering to the Highest
Truth.

Aquinas clearly recognizes the twofold activity of the
divine image in us when he affirms that "the commandments of natural law sometimes are actually adverted to by
the reason and sometimes just settled convictions there" in
human nature.[33] *Synderesis* is a quasi-*habitus* which offers
the first principles of the *practical* reason. This *habitus*

forms a companion with *intellectus*, or understanding, which serves a similar purpose for the *speculative* intellect. Some authors, lacking such precisions, even call *synderesis* the law of our understanding, to the extent that it amounts to the *habitus* of keeping the precepts of the natural law. These precepts, of course, constitute the first principles of human activity, so that *synderesis* actually starts the process of transforming the inclinations of the *imago* into working principles for concrete moral activity.[34] Of course, the practical principle that good is to be sought and done and evil is to be avoided forms only the basis or starting point for the development of right conduct.

Acquired moral learning plays an important role in this development. At the level of the appetitive, the common principles of natural law remain settled convictions ordered towards the basic goods of human flourishing.[35] However, at the rational level of properly discursive human knowledge, *synderesis* contributes by offering the first principles to the development of practical moral knowledge through the work of prudence and its integral parts.[36] Prudence, then, integrates moral knowledge and rectified appetites to provide concrete, particular norms for human behavior. All of the moral virtues require prudence because this virtue alone guarantees the actual production of virtuous behavior, not simply the knowledge of what to do. Prudence promises that when correct moral reasoning combines with rectified appetite for good ends, a virtuous action inevitably results.

The scholastics called these good ends the "thing" or *res* of nature.[37] So that detraction, for example, destroys the *res* of human social life and communication in the same way that a contagious disease harms the *res* of public health. On the other hand, prudential conformity with a *res* of human flourishing produces a virtuous person who easily and surely achieves that perfection of human life. Unlike the good musician who, in order to instruct a student, may deliberately play a false note, the prudent person cannot voluntarily act imprudently. One cannot hypothetically set aside what prudence teaches. For the cardinal virtue of prudence ultimately shapes the person in such a way that acting properly, as St. Paul reminds the Corinthians, results from a new or second nature. "Therefore, if any one is in Christ, he is a new creation; the old has passed away, behold, the new has come" (2 Cor 5:17).

PRUDENCE AND MORAL KNOWLEDGE

Yet, even as it shares in the perfection of the moral virtues in commanding a virtuous mean and, therefore, the realization of a moral action, prudence remains an intellectual virtue. Thus, the first principles of practical reason, held by *synderesis*, develop into a large body of specific moral knowledge. Recall that prudence particularizes moral truth for application to concrete cases. Although the precision of moral learning varies in different people, the ethicist can isolate at least three discrete moments in the development of moral consciousness. These moments occur in each mature individual no matter what stage of intellectual advancement the person has attained.

(1) Basic moral reflection. This amounts to the pre-scientific grasp of general moral principles which results from ordinary human experience: for example, the principle that each one receives a just share of common goods.

(2) Moral science. The reasoned, organized development of this reflection into a coherent body of truths: for example, Rawls' theory of justice. In fact, any ethical theory attempts to formulate moral science.

(3) Conscience. The application of general or developed moral principles to an individual's singular action either about to be done or already accomplished: for example, here and now I should pay (or should have paid) $1,000 to the federal government for income tax.

It should be emphasized, however, that moral knowledge, which differs from speculative knowledge because of the practical end it pursues, belongs to the order of action. Since the contingency of human events impairs a fully accurate prediction of outcomes, a practical science produces scientific results only in the broad sense.

Three distinct acts embody prudence's principal working. These are counsel, judgment, and command. Counsel, shaped by the special virtue of *eubulia*, supplies a rational deliberation about means which ensures that the prudent person solicits whatever established moral wisdom provides for a certain matter. Judgment makes a decision about what one is going to do now; it follows the settling onto concrete means. The practical judgment of conscience applies this particularized wisdom to the actual circumstances of a given case. If a poorly informed conscience makes a faulty judgment about particulars, no virtue can develop; the question of culpability, however, raises other questions. Because of the importance the act of judgment holds in the moral life, two special virtues aid its formation: *synesis* ensures sound judgment in ordinary matters and *gnome* provides the wit to judge the exceptional cases. Finally, command supplies the efficacious imperative note in the act of prudence. To command remains the principal act of prudence which gives to the judgment of conscience its imperative value. By this, prudence enters into the formal act of the moral virtues, i.e., the choosing of the good as such.

The goal of seeking conformity between the human person and the good moral ends of human flourishing requires the *dictamen* or "saying" of conscience. For conscience, the act of the intellect which most immediately affects free choice, serves as the final instance of applied moral truth. Although it brings the full weight of formed moral truth to bear on decision, conscience does not constitute choice. Moral theories which rely exclusively on conscience restrict the parameters within which moral decision making occurs. Such theories exhibit a mistrust of nature and experience as an authentic source of moral wisdom. The cardinal virtue of prudence, however, provides both the ability for making concrete moral decisions and, at the same time, ensures that these decisions actually satisfy human nature created after the *imago Dei*. Practical moral knowledge, then, easily leads to theological reflection. In fact, theology—being a certain impression in us of the knowledge which God shares with the blessed in heaven—qualifies as a practical science. "St. John of the Cross and St. Alphonsus," observes Jacques Maritain, "were able to produce absolutely sure practical doctrine not only because they were learned but also prudent and experienced."[38]

Prudence and Action

Prudence, even though a virtue of the mind, operates differently than the virtues of the speculative intellect, wisdom, science, and understanding. Aquinas emphasizes that the perfect correctness of reason in speculative matters depends upon the principles from which it argues. For example, speculative science depends on and presupposes understanding, which is the *habitus* of its principles. "In human acts, however, ends are what principles are in speculative matters, as stated in the *Ethics* [7, 1151a16]. Consequently, prudence, which is right reason about things to be done, requires that a man be rightly disposed with regard to ends; and this depends on rightness of appetite."[39] Prudence operates only in connection with the inclinations of the human person to achieve a well-defined moral end. In this, moral realism differs from ethical rationalism which begins with wholly abstract principles or "rules" of reasoning and regards the objectives of particular virtues as secondary and relative.

Although prudence is a virtue of the practical intellect, it also differs from art. The distinction between art and prudence offers the most helpful insight into its uniqueness.

Philosophers consider art a virtue of the practical intellect since it produces the capacity, by means of a *habitus*, for the artist to make something properly. Art, according to a realist aesthetics, finds its norm or measure in an object which exists outside of the virtue's own principles. For example, the person who sits for a portrait is the measure of the work of the artist who produces it. Art, then, seeks to represent that which exists outside itself, even if, as happens with abstract forms, the measure exists principally in the imagination of the artist. Prudence, on the other hand, works differently for it must discover the measure for a moral act within its own structure, as this measure depends on the actual state of one's appetites. In other words, prudence incorporates personal experience into its own *habitus* formation. Thus, in order to function as a directive truth for moral action, acquired prudence presupposes that a person has learned from human experience something about right dispositions.[40]

The term "human experience" has been made to carry considerable theological weight in recent decades. Theologians influenced by Marxist thought find the category fruitful for theological analysis and critique, as did authors involved in the Modernist crisis at the turn of the century.[41] It would be unfortunate if reaction to these schools of thought resulted in a wholesale rejection of such an important element in Christian moral theology. For the moral theologian, human experience entails the proper interaction between the human subject and a world of created realities, i.e., specific objects of experience. In turn, these objects make up the particular configuration of one's moral universe for weal or woe.[42]

The congruity which exists between human nature and the objects capable of satisfying its needs is called the order of intention. An end-in-intention (*finis in intentione*) develops precisely because human nature seeks to complete itself by moving towards and embracing those good objects which comprise its well-being.[43] The obvious examples include such things as food, truth, sexual gratification, but other goods such as friendship, personal accomplishment, integrity, play, and so forth also constitute objects which become ends-in-intention for us.[44] Again, realist moral theology trusts both nature and experience as contributing to the development of moral wisdom. For example, everyone recognizes that materials which the human body cannot assimilate fail to qualify as foodstuffs. Rocks simply do not fit nature's digestive system in the way an authentic moral object, such as Peking duck, must do in order to serve as an end-in-intention for humans. Of course, good instruction can spare one the chagrin of having to learn by experience about such inappropriate objects.

The moral virtues ensure in principle that we are disposed to pursue only honorable ends-in-intention. Consider the futility of seeking sound moral judgment about sobriety from one who habitually drinks too much. Why is this so? The answer lies in the way such a person has made bourbon or beer an end. In this sense, each one acts in accord with the way he or she intends, i.e., regards, a given end of human life. For the drunkard, this is a disordered attachment to drink. A scholastic adage summarizes this truth: *qualis sum secundum appetitum meum, talis mihi videtur finis.*[45] In other words, the shape of one's emotional life actually dictates how an individual will discriminate among a range of options, and consequently, if asked, will give advice to others. Disordered desires obviously affect the practical judgment an individual makes about the use of certain goods, about how he or she approaches an intended end. Accordingly, the miser wants only more money; the profligate seeks more sexual gratification; the glutton more food, and so forth. These are the carnal sinners, as Dante calls them in the *Inferno*, "who subject reason to desire."[46]

Still, disordered appetite can affect prudence only in an indirect way. For command, the proper act of prudence itself, originates in the intellect. Aquinas expresses this

truth with utmost clarity: "A commander orders a subor-
dinate to do something, and his order is conveyed by way
of imitation or declaration. This is a function of reason."[47]
Although moral theologians of a voluntarist bent raise
questions such as whether God could change his will about
divine commands, this kind of speculation holds no interest
for the moral realist. For in the final analysis, moral realism
measures moral truth according to the likeness of divine
wisdom which exists in the created order. In other terms,
prudence looks to introduce the *veritas vitae*, the truth
about life, into the world. Within this context, we can
appreciate the important role which the Church's Magisterium plays in giving proper direction to moral conduct.
Recent instructions on matters as diverse as prayer and
bioethics indicate the range of moral topics which require
clarification from a competent "lawmaker" in light of revealed truth.

PRUDENCE AND DIVINE PROVIDENCE

Prudence puts good moral reasoning into a virtuous action. Upon entering Hell, Virgil reminds Dante that he is
about to see the "woeful people who have lost the good of
the intellect."[48] As a process of discursive reasoning, then,
we can suggest a parallel between prudence and the speculative syllogism of formal logic. Speculative reasoning unfolds in two basic moments: first, the seizure of the first
principles of speculative thought through the *habitus* of
understanding; and, secondly, a series of subsequent acts
of judgment and reasoning from which conclusions are developed. A significant difference, however, arises in the case
of the practical syllogism which directs human behavior.
Since the end result of practical reasoning is doing the
truth, not just knowing it, practical reasoning must con-
front certain existential complexities. For example, no
moral science can ensure the truthfulness of the conclusion

"I should not take this drink, now, under these conditions, at this moment." Rather, moral science can only establish the general principle that drunkenness embodies a defective end for human life; reason alone cannot supply the actual virtue—actually to refrain from that amount of bourbon or beer which causes drunkenness.

On the other hand, good moral theory should offer no place for the Stoic doctrine of *apatheia*, that is, a cultivated disregard for one's emotional state. Indeed, moral development necessarily implies emotional maturity. Moral virtue tempers, but does not suppress the emotional life. Theories which suppose the will's supremacy over the emotional life treat the emotions as if they were unruly slaves in need of despotic control. Such repression of emotion, thought it may seem virtuous to some, amounts in effect to a miming of virtue. On the contrary, prudence treats the emotions as friends within the city of reason precisely because these sense powers above all need the discipline of moral truth. Aquinas sagely remarks, "Not all moral virtues are about delight and sorrow, as their proper matter but. . . . every virtuous person delights in an act of virtue and is saddened by an act contrary to virtue."[49]

Prudence is an intellectual virtue; its principal concern remains objective moral truth. It can only reach completion in the concrete affairs of life when the moral virtues, which steady the movement of the appetites, supply prudence with the right ends-in-intention.[50] As the emotions can always rebel against reason, prudence depends on the moral virtues in order even to dispose emotions rightly with regard to their proper ends. Once, however, this synergy of right reason and right appetite, shaped by the virtues of justice, fortitude, and temperance, has taken place, human actions commanded by prudence perfectly embody moral goodness. When this occurs, the prudent man or woman can also be said to possess certain knowledge that this particular choice here and now wholly achieves the virtue of *veritas vitae*. In this way, divine providence ensures that it governs all things gently.

All the virtues of the Christian life enable the believer to make this evangelical verity an effective part of his or her life. Because God's truth is simple, that is, undivided, a single virtue in the intellect can serve to inform us about how to pursue a variety of moral goods to be pursued and evils to be avoided. On the other hand, it is clear that many different kinds of moral good exist in the world. Therefore, although all moral actions require but a single cognitive *habitus* for proper operation, the variety of moral goods available to the human person means that he or she needs a multiplicity of moral virtues.[51] The moral virtues fall into two general categories.[52] First, the moral virtues which regulate the emotional life (*circa passiones*) include the cardinal virtues of fortitude and temperance and their allied virtues. Second, the cardinal virtue of justice which regulates one's activity towards other human persons, either individually or in community, and toward God (*circa operationes*), includes the virtues of veneration and respect. So while the cardinal virtues specify generic kinds of virtue, they also serve as focal points for laying out clusters of other virtues. These moral virtues form our human capacities in a variety of specific ways, so that virtue theory adequately addresses every particular situation in the moral life.

Voluntarists may prefer to speak of God's will as the chief factor which determines right moral practice, but moral realism looks to divine providence as a source of moral direction for each man and woman. Prudence extends divine providence so that it reaches even to the most particular of moral actions. A true Christian personalism must maintain that nothing which transpires in human affairs lies outside of God's loving care. "Therefore I tell you, do not be anxious about your life, what you shall eat, nor about your body, what you shall put on," Jesus warns his disciples. "Consider the ravens: they neither sow nor reap, they have neither storehouse nor barn, and yet God feeds them. O how much more value are you than the birds! And which of you by being anxious can add a cubit to his span?" (Lk 12:22,24–25).

5. WHAT CAUSES THE MORAL VIRTUES TO DEVELOP

MORAL VIRTUE AND THE THEOLOGICAL LIFE

The pages of the New Testament repeatedly emphasize that the actual happiness of the believer results from a sustained union with the crucified and risen Christ. Jesus himself points out that remaining united with him requires a special action of divine providence in the life of those called to Christian belief. The Gospel of John, for example, puts these words on the lips of Christ: "No one can come to me unless the Father who sent me draws him; and I will raise him up on the last day" (Jn 6:44). Of course, since many other spiritual benefits result from the union of the believer with Christ, one cannot simply equate the whole effect of incorporation into Christ with the practice of virtue. Still, the moral life does remain a principal area where the presence of grace makes itself felt in the individual, especially through the theological virtues. For a variety of reasons, theologians today generally do not speak about the theological virtues of faith, hope, and charity as constitutive elements of the moral life. On the contrary, prevailing theological method prefers to study these virtues as special topics in either systematic or biblical theology.

Neglect of the theological virtues in moral theology remains regrettable for several reasons. First, each theological virtue possesses its own objective interest which it develops in the one who possesses the particular *habitus*. Faith engages the believer with the content of Christian revelation; hope with the concrete means for achieving what faith promises; and, charity with everything worthy of authentic Christian love. Secondly, and what perhaps is more important, each of the theological virtues unites the believer to God in a specific way. Faith unites the believer to God the First Truth; hope to God who is Highest Good for me; and charity to God who is Highest Good in himself. This union, rooted in habitual grace, amounts to a real and active relationship between the persons of the blessed Trinity and the one living the theological life. Although the tradition usually speaks about this indwelling as a work of the Holy Spirit, the believer actually enjoys a proper relationship with each of the indwelling divine Persons. Accordingly, the theological virtues ensure that the Christian moral life remains radically distinct from mere ethical culture. When the theological virtues animate the life of the believer, the moral energies of the human person, including the fundamental resolve to live a virtuous life, originate and find their sustaining power in the triune God. Sometimes, in fact, the theological virtues are called divine virtues. Aquinas explains the practice, "These virtues are called divine not as though by them God is virtuous, but rather because by them God makes us virtuous and directs us to him."[1]

Of course, the theological virtues only account for part of the graced moral life of the believer. There exists a difference in the moral life between the acquired virtues and those which the theological tradition designates as infused. The Christian tradition judges that a complete account of the development of virtue in the life of the believer requires examination of at least two efficient causes: on the one hand, human activity in itself and, on the other hand, a special divine action, which, since it involves the graced development of a *habitus*, theologians call "infusion."[2] When asked to explain why a believer would require virtues other than the theological ones in order to live a complete Christian life, Aquinas replied: "The theological virtues order us sufficiently to a supernatural end in an incipient way, that is, to God himself. Other infused virtues, however, are needed to perfect the soul with respect to other things, but in relation to God."³

VIRTUES IN NATURE

As even the early Christian apologists argued, the Gospel *paideia,* or instruction, requires that an individual develop a distinctive moral culture. Therefore, Christian theology can never endorse the Enlightenment position that untutored human nature represents the best expression of the race. Of course, Diderot, in the *Supplement to Bougainville's Voyage,* tried to distinguish between those desires which are natural in the species and those artificially formed and corrupted desires which civilization breeds in us. Although he professed to believe that basic human nature is both uncovered in and served by what he imagined as the promiscuous sexuality of certain Polynesians, his actual moral practice (for example, in the upbringing of his daughter) revealed the usual concerns of the *bon bourgeois* about marriage, truth-telling, and so forth.⁴ In fact, for most French Enlightenment thinkers, despite their optimistic theoretical views about unvarnished human nature elsewhere, Paris in actual practice fully realized their vision of the Heavenly City. Christian thinkers, such as Aquinas, save themselves both the embarrassment and disappointment in which such a naive view of human nature inevitably results. Because they note the actual circumstances of the world, realist theologians are ready to accept the plainly evident fact that original sin touches each individual. Aquinas explains: "As a result of [the loss of original justice] all the powers of the soul are in a sense lacking an order proper to them, their natural order to virtue, and the deprivation is called the wounding of nature."⁵ Aquinas shares this realist estimate of the human condition with other

Christian thinkers who, from the start of the second century, developed the implications of the biblical doctrine of original sin.

Anthropological factors argue against the existence of built-in virtues in human nature. *Habitus* development requires the possibility of achieving a particular end by means of diverse modes of activity. Accordingly, were a virtue established in nature in such wise that the will would always act in accordance with prudence just as, given the presence of light, the healthy eye always sees any colored object, the versatility of authentically human behavior would be sacrificed in favor of what could only amount to some form of innate determinism. Some continental rationalists may have wished this were the case, but their explanations usually resulted in depreciating human liberty in favor of an artificially imposed world order. Leibniz's *Monadology* proposes something like this when it speaks about "pre-arranged harmony."[6] At least, Diderot imagined a more exciting and varied life for his "virtuous" Polynesians. Still, both rationalist and romantic views must consistently spar with reality, instead of interpreting the plain evidence human experience supplies.

When it comes to evaluating basic human nature, Christian realism seeks to maintain a balanced position. It can never suggest that human nature, even in its fallen state, amounts to a miserable wreck left only to await divine intervention in order to realize any moral goodness whatsoever. Still, it must recognize that the grace of redemption, which heals the disorder caused by the loss of original justice, alone ensures that anyone can sustain a vigorous moral life for any period of time. On the other hand, moral realists surely reject the Pelagian view that, given the fact of Christ's resurrection, human nature's inclination to virtue itself suffices to lead a morally good life. Why? According to the classical conception of the actual state of the human condition, original sin results in a privation of original justice for everyone born into the world. As a result, our human powers remain wounded in being deprived of right moral order until such time as the individual, moved by divine grace and baptized into the Body of Christ, begins freely to meet the requirements of Christian virtue.[7] Yet, even in the state of fallen nature, an instinct for virute remains.

There does exist a sense in which the expression "natural virtue" can be understood by the Christian theologian. This amounts to a distinguishable tendency within human nature to achieve its own perfection and to live in accord with right reason. Human nature manifests this instinct for its own virtuous perfection both at the level of specific nature, that is, the nature shared by each member of the human species, and at the level of individuated nature, that is, the way each member of the race concretely possesses a particular embodiment of common nature. Philosophers usually distinguish an individual instance of human nature, divided off from other members who share the same nature by a distinct amount of physical matter, from the full and complete realization of that nature for which they reserve the special term, the person.[8] Aquinas allows for natural virtue in the individual "insofar as by certain bodily dispositions some are disposed better or worse to certain virtues."[9] He goes on to explain:

> Virtue is natural to us in respect to specific nature insofar as certain naturally known principles in regard to both thought [*intellectus*] and action [*synderesis*] are in our reason naturally, which are like the seeds of intellectual and moral virtue, and insofar as there is in the will a certain appetite for good in conformity with reason.[10]

Aquinas recognizes the existence of a more general instinct for virtue as a given of the human reality, but he also insists that every human nature requires moral development in order to develop these instincts, which, admittedly, may or may not be easily formed in the right way.

ACQUIRED VIRTUE

Acquired virtue provides one way for human nature to develop. Obviously a single action cannot produce the kind of permanent disposition in our psychological structure which constitutes a *habitus*. The development of *habitus* requires a series of repeated actions. But how much repetition does virtue require in order for a person to feel secure in its possession? Aristotle felt that the responsibility for developing virtue could not be left to the majority of people. Rather, he argued, a good legislator should see to it that the right kind of habituation goes on among the citizens.[11] Christian philosophy adopts a more personalist approach to virtue formation, one which respects an individual's freedom and abilities. Yves Simon reflects this approach when he discusses some of the variables involved in the development of *habitus*.

> Again, the number of repetitions required to establish a habit varies greatly from person to person, as well as from case to case. How many times do you have to smoke marijuana to develop the habit? How many times do you have to take opium? I personally would not want to experiment with any of that stuff, because you never know. Do we know how many readings it takes to memorize a poem? Does it take more to memorize texts in a foreign language? Nonsense verse? It all depends on the person. Speaking in general, we know that it takes younger people less time to do it than it takes older people. Moreover, some rare individuals can get anything committed to memory by glancing at it just once. But these are exceptions to the rule. The law of habit calls for repetition.[12]

Although the author enunciates commonsense rules for the development of an acquired virtue, repetition by itself does not account for the growth of a virtuous *habitus*.

The repetition of disordered actions, it is true, can develop a vice, but repetition, Aquinas insists, produces vir-

tue only "insofar as acts of such virtue proceed from reason, under whose power and rule such good is
established."[13] The development of virtue also demands
that one observe the requirements which right reason establishes for any given virtue. One can not develop, for
example, the virtue of chastity by following whatsoever
norm for personal conduct in matters of sexual comportment. Nor does one arrive at the stabilization that virtue
requires by experimenting with different measures for a
chaste life, such as those guidelines suggested by people
who hold diverse views about the purposes of human sexuality. This would amount to employing different "rules"
for measuring virture, and, as a result, no single *habitus*
would develop. Rather, acquired virtue must hold a steady
course in accord with the unique truth of the Eternal Law.
This does not mean that the repeated actions need remain
monotonously the same. To the extent that prudence plays
its role in the moral life, the particular realization of moral
truth in a given instance will always represent something
new and fresh. At the same time, authentic prudence, since
it depends ultimately on the Eternal Law, guarantees that
each action it commands contains the full measure of moral
truth.[14] This, in turn, ensures that one acquires a single
virtue.

Once developed, acquired virtue enjoys all of the qualities which belong to *habitus*. These virtues embody stable
dispositions for operation which shape the powers of the
human person to achieve a specifically good kind of activity. Aristotle observes that virtue is sometimes regarded as
"a faculty of providing and preserving good things."[15] As a
result, the one who possesses an acquired virtue attains a
particular good of human nature, such as steadfastness in
the face of difficulties, towards which the virtue—in this
example, fortitude—strives. Furthermore, the acquired virtue enables the one who develops it to act after the fashion
of an *habitus*-formed act, that is, promptly, easily, and with
a measure of satisfaction and joy.

The brave person exhibits a decided readiness to respond to a threatening situation and, in the midst of facing up to whatever dangers the situation poses, such a one betrays the kind of steady confidence which only comes after repeated satisfactory experiences of this kind. If the circumstances allow, the brave person can even realize the pleasant sensations which usually accompany performing a familiar but worthwhile task, although at certain other times, as Aquinas observes, it is enough that the virtuous person act without sadness.[16] Similar examples could be offered for each of the moral virtues. Virtue establishes in us a kind of second nature, since it provides a steady inclination for freely performing good actions in the same way nature itself operates with respect to necessary actions, such as sight and digestion. But even acquired virtue, since it observes the general rules of *habitus* development and operation, respects the person's freedom in determining the conditions for peforming or refraining from a particular action.

In discussion about the acquired virtues, questions arise: What happens when one who possesses an acquired virtue commits a sin? How does a vicious act affect the virtuous *habitus*? Of course, even an acquired *habitus* can diminish in intensity and, eventually, disappear.[17] But just as the development of the acquired virtue requires a certain number of repeated actions, so also its loss requires a certain number of contrary actions. Thus, sin affects acquired virtue differently than it does the infused moral virutes for the latter are not compatible with mortal sin, in other words, the loss of charity. Why? The answer lies in the special relationship that exists between the infused virtues and the life of faith. Since the infused virtues rely on the graced relationship between the believer and Christ, a decisive rupture in that relationship, such as one caused by serious sin, can only result in the effective loss of the infused virtues. But acquired virtue functions differently, for the acquired moral virtues remain compatible with a single sinful or vicious act, even a grave one.

Aquinas offers two reasons for this. First, he explains that the use of an acquired *habitus* remains subject to our willing, even if, at that moment, we are not actually loving God. In other words, the soldier, who sees that the good and honorable thing to do is to stand and fight, thereby risking death, does not necessarily require sanctifying grace to do so; or, the citizen, who pays income taxes, thereby fulfilling the norms of legal justice, may not, on that account, enjoy the intimacy of divine friendship. A second reason why one sinful act does not destroy an acquired virtue involves the nature of a *habitus*. Only another developed *habitus*, which a single action cannot generate, is contrary to an acquired *habitus*.[18] Although personal sin always remains in a serious matter, it does not, at least initially, destroy whatever acquired virtues the individual may have developed. This explains Aquinas's optimistic teaching on the moral life, namely, that "although without grace one cannot avoid mortal sin, so as never to sin mortally, yet one is not hindered from acquiring a *habitus* of virtue whereby one can abstain from evil deeds for the most part, and especially from those which are very much opposed to reason."[19]

INFUSED VIRTUE

The theory that, in addition to the theological virtues, there also exists a group of infused moral virtues enjoys a long tradition in the history of theology. The medieval schoolmen, influenced by the Augustinian view that the virtues of the philosophers counted for nothing towards salvation, accepted the infusion of the moral virtues as a given of Christian teaching. Writers from the period of high scholasticism, such as Philip the Chancellor, John de la Rochelle, Albert the Great, and Odo Rigaud, each of whom devoted long treatises to the moral virtues, passed over the question of whether they were infused or not. They simply took the matter for granted.[20] Yet towards the end of the thirteenth century, certain theologians, even some who were students in Paris during the time Aquinas lectured on the infused virtues, took exception to the practice of speaking about the infused virtues as distinct *habitus* within the Christian life. Duns Scotus undoubtedly best summarizes the reasoning behind this position. In his *Quaestiones in librum Sententiarum* he disputed the necessity of the infused virtues:

> Although many things are said about these infused moral virtues, in particular, that they are necessary on account of a [supernatural] mode, mean, and end, in fact there seems no reason to hold for infused moral virtues, rather the acquired virtues suffice. Why? First, because any end, not already provided for in nature, can be adequately supplied as a result of the inclination of charity. Secondly, because infused faith supplies the required mode and mean for virtue.[21]

Thus, Scotus introduces the major features of the alternative explanation with regard to how grace actually effects a change in the moral life of the believer.[22]

Others would follow Scotus's lead in this matter, seeing charity and faith as providing a permanent influence on the moral virtues, with the result that believer and non-believer alike possess only those virtues acquired by the repetition of human actions. Charity, as Scotus observed, transforms the acquired virtues into real forms of loving God. Faith supplies the necessary information in order to establish the special mode and mean that a virtue of Christian perfection requires. Thus, for example, one would learn from faith that the mean of acquired abstinence in food differs on a day set aside for fasting, or that infused conjugal chastity excludes certain practices between a husband and wife which otherwise might appear to fit the "mode" of the acquired virtue.[23] But the acquired virtues themselves, in-

sofar as they possess a psychological structure, remain unchanged. The Scotistic position exhibits clear similarities
with the way contemporary theologians, to the extent they
consider the theological virtues at all, describe the function
of faith and charity in the moral life.[24]

For Aquinas, however, such an account does not suffice
to explain how divine grace affects the moral life of one
who practices the Christian faith. Citing Wisdom 8:7, "She
[i.e., Wisdom] teaches temperance and prudence and justice and fortitude," Aquinas responds in the affirmative to
the question: "Are any moral virtues infused in us?"

> Effects must be proportionate to their causes and principles.
> Now all virtues, intellectual and moral, which are acquired
> by our actions, proceed from certain natural principles which
> pre-exist in us, as we have said [in q. 51, a.1]. In place of
> these natural principles, God has bestowed on us theological
> virtues whereby we are ordered to a supernatural end, as we
> have also said [in q. 62, a.1]. Hence it was necessary that
> other *habitus*, corresponding proportionately to the theologi-
> cal virtues, be caused in us by God which are related to the
> theological virtues as the moral and intellectual virtues are to
> the natural principles of virtue.[25]

Since so much of what remains distinctive in Aquinas's
moral theology rests on this affirmation, the text of this
response merits a close reading.

First, consider the kind of theological reasoning which
guides the development of the argument. Certain truths of
the faith are set in relationship to one another so that some
new conclusion emerges, making explicit what remains implicit in a general principle. The vocation of the Christian
believer to participate in the divine life serves as the starting
principle, a premise, for the argument concerning the existence of the infused virtues. Since divine love only follows
upon divine initiative, this participation in God's very life
amounts to something entirely above nature's abilities. "For
it belongs to his limitless power," writes Aquinas, "to bring

us to limitless good. Such a good is life eternal, consisting in the joyful possession of God himself."[26] Because it stands outside of the created order, we can correctly refer to this "joyful possession" as a supernatural state. God remains "above" nature only in the sense that his sheer transcendence escapes any real relationship to creation. Although, as the doctrine of creation *ex nihilo* makes clear, creation really depends on him.

Beatitude, then, constitutes the only complete state of human happiness. The dilemma which this faith affirmation embodies continues to provide grist for theologians' mills. Thomas Gilby succinctly sets forth the paradox: First, that man has been created by God in his nature and natural powers, not as a heartless joke, but with some natural expectancy of such development that he will reach to his fulfillment or happiness. Second, that this end can be reached only by the pure gift of grace quite beyond his deserving by any natural efforts of his own.[27] Classical realist theology argues further that since the human mind can not encompass this "limitless good," the human will cannot naturally desire it. And the Pastoral Constitution on the Church in the Modern World expresses a similar point of view: "Imagination is completely helpless when confronted with death. Yet the Church, instructed by divine revelation, affirms that man has been created by God for a destiny of happiness beyond the reach of earthly trials."[28]

Thus, when Aquinas affirms that "there can be no complete and final happiness for us save in the vision of God,"[29] he proposes beatitude both as the ultimate goal or end of the Christian life as well as the Archimedean point around which the infused virtues operate in the moral life. Aquinas's argument for the infused virtues continues then with a premise of reason, namely, the psychological principle that there should exist in the human person a capacity proportionate for any given human activity. Intelligent discourse, for example, requires an intellect in the same way that Christian hoping requires a will. If the moral life could rest in something created, such as, the establishment of a just society or the display of a courageous heroism, the human person would already possess, in nature, the capacities required to achieve such perfection. But because the authentic happiness of the human person requires more than this, despite the claims to the contrary of secular humanism—claims advanced in both politics and psychology—each one of us requires additional capacities. Only the power of the Holy Spirit can create capacities proportionate to attaining supernatural beatitude. Besides the theological virtues, then, these divinely established capacities include the infused moral virtues. In like manner, St. Paul evokes the infused moral virtues when he reminds the backsliding Galatians: "For through the Spirit, by faith, we wait for the hope of righteousness (Gal 5:5).

The infused moral virtues assume that God has acted in human history in such a way as to make beatific fellowship with himself possible for every member of the race.[30] This elevation of human nature's destiny requires a proportionate elevation of human nature's capacities. The divergent schools of opinion on the infused virtues agree about the transformation of human destiny, yet they disagree, in effect, about the explicit difference this makes for the theological life. Take a simple example, the virtue of abstinence. Moderation with respect to one's consumption of food can obviously serve a natural end, such as the maintenance of health and hygiene. The same moderation, however, can also serve to unite one more closely with Christ and the sufferings of his members, for example, when one fasts during Lent. In both instances the activity involved, namely, eating less, remains the same. But for the believer, fasting for Christ's sake involves something altogether new and different for it introduces what theologians call a new formal measure or mean. According to this new formal measure, admittedly established only by faith, grace molds the believer for activity which reaches directly to God.

To be sure, some authors argue that one can adequately explain an infused virtue by simply adding on, as it were, a motive derived from charity to an already existing acquired virtue. According to this line of interpretation, the dieter who starts to fast for Christ's sake simply adds a new motive, albeit supernatural, to the already existing *habitus*. Thus, although one's charity may devleop, for such a person the moral virtue of abstinence, considered as a distinct operative *habitus*, remains unchanged. While granting that the explanation offers an attractively easy way out of what can become a complex issue, its shortcoming lies in describing growth in the Christian moral life exclusively in terms of charity. The very importance the New Testament's message assigns to the love of God and neighbor requires that other virtues besides the theological reflect the radical change grace effects in the whole human person.

The scholastic theologians, with a precision characteristic of their trade, described this effect of charity on a believer's moral life as a change *quoad modum tendendi in finem supernaturalem*. To put it differently, charity affects the direction, but not the substance of an action whereby the believer reaches out towards God. Charity, then, affects the doer's intention—in the strong sense of substantial purpose, not the weak sense of sporadic motive.[31] Charity cannot account for why one act of abstinence embodies an intrinsic difference not found in another act of abstinence. Yet, since fasting in union with the Mystical Body counts as a distinctive feature of the Christian moral life, the *habitus* which makes the fasting possible should itself include an intrinsic reference to grace. Accordingly, only a distinct virtue, the infused virtue of abstinence, can fully account for the total reality caused in the believer by the working of the Holy Spirit. The only alternative to affirming the existence of the infused virtue remains considering the action of grace as limited to altering the purposes, but not the habits of the heart. The Letter to the Hebrews surely promises more than this, when, quoting Jeremiah 31:31, it describes the effects of the new dispensation: "This is the covenant that I will make with the house of Israel after those days, says the Lord: I will put my laws into their minds, and write them on their hearts, and I will be their God, and they shall be my people" (Heb. 8:10).

As one author put it, this may seem like a needless multiplication of virtues to some people, but Ockham's razor does not cut here.[32] The infused virtues do not constitute superfluous extras calculated to make theology's task more difficult than it would be if it did not have to deal with a whole special category of virtues. Rather, the existence of the infused virtues reveals God's providential plan whereby he chooses to endow the order of grace with the same kind of provisions already established for the order of nature. Recall that the infused moral virtues include authentically graced activities. As a result, the one who acts with such a *habitus* actually participates in the merits of Christ's sacrificial death and resurrection. The infused virtues belong to the kind of life lived in the Church of faith and sacraments. The Letter to the Ephesians expresses this well when, addressing the newly converted Gentiles, it recalls a time when they were once "separated from Christ, alienated from the commonwealth of Israel, and strangers to the covenants of promise, having no hope and without God in the world. But now in Christ Jesus you who once were far off have been brought near in the blood of Christ" (Eph 2:11–14). The reality of the infused virtues implies that the Christian moral life possesses all the characteristics of an intrinsic morality, though transformed by the power of faith.

Thus, when Jesus restored sight to the eyes of the man born blind, the capacity for seeing, even though restored by a miracle, remains a natural one.[33] Similarly, when a philanthropist gives money to a good cause, the action, even though a worthwhile one, remains an exercise of acquired virtue. Only grace can transform it into an expression of Gospel life, namely, the infused virtue of magnificence.[34] The realization of Gospel values only results from a thoroughgoing transformation of both the believer and his or her actions. When this happens, the distinctiveness of New Testament morality appears, not because Christians do the same good things as everyone else, though with an eye towards loving God, but because a totally new form has been given by faith to the virtuous deed. Christ's teaching about the widow's offering surely reflects this mystery. The Gospel of Luke recounts that when Jesus saw a poor widow, in the company of the rich, put two copper coins into the container to receive offerings, he declared: "Truly I tell you, this poor widow has put in more than all of them; for they all contributed out of their abundance, but she out of her poverty put in all the living that she had" (Lk 21:1–4).

HOW TO DISTINGUISH INFUSED FROM ACQUIRED VIRTUE

Drawing a distinction between acquired and infused virtues in the climate of contemporary Christian ethics appears to separate out Christian morality from the ethical demands accessible, at least in principle, to rational insight apart from revelation.[35] The medieval theologians, to the extent that they possessed a unified cosmic view of grace and nature, recognized that all worldly activity possesses significance, however potential, for salvation. They did not, however, distill pure forms of human nature and natural morality out of whatever concrete, historical shape divine grace gave to them. Since beatific union with God remains the only actual ultimate end for human existence, the theologian must maintain that both acquired and infused virtues compose an organic unity, as it were, in the believer. On this evidence, Aquinas sought to distinguish between acquired and infused virtues on the twofold basis of measure and purpose.

First, Aquinas describes the difference between the acquired and infused virtues on the basis of the different purposes which they accomplish: "The acquired virtues direct civil life whence they have the civil good as an end. The infused moral virtues, on the other hand, perfect the spiritual life, insofar as one belongs, as a citizen, to the City of God and, as a member, to the Body of Christ, which is the Church."[36] Furthermore, since ends serve as principles for the development of virtue, the express purpose of the infused virtues requires that their starting points also differ from those of the acquired virtues.

> Acquired virtues specifically differ from infused virtues, for example, fortitude from fortitude, temperance from temperance, and so on with the other virtues. The reason? In matters of practical reason, ends serve the function of principles. Accordingly, were some science not able to be reduced to naturally known principles, it would not be included within the same species as the other sciences, nor referred to, at least univocally, as a science. This happens with the infused virtues, since their ends are not contained within the natural seeds of virtue. Thus the requirement for specifically distinguishing the infused virtues from the acquired virtues which, in fact, do arise out of these seeds. The infused virtues, moreover, perfect a person for a different kind of life. In brief, the acquired virtues ready one for civil life, but the infused for a spiritual life, which comes only from grace as a result of the virtuous one's membership in the Church.[37]

As they derive from divine grace, the infused virtues form specifically distinct *habitus* from their acquired analogues.

Secondly, the infused virtues observe a different norm or measure from that established for the virtues of the human community. Obviously, this different norm or measure amounts to more than simply supplying the political virtues, as Aquinas sometimes refers to the acquired virtues, with a charitable intention. At the same time, the difference between the infused and acquired virtues does not mean that the latter follow a hypothetical pure natural norm of reason and the former an equally hypothetical pure supernatural norm of revelation.[38] Realist moral theology provides a more sophisticated explanation of how diverse standards of measure affect the two kinds of virtues. In order to grasp it, one must recall the general distinction between form and matter as this applies to the virtues.

Consider, for example, Aquinas's proposal that acts of infused virtues and acts of the acquired virtues remain one and the same *"materialiter."* For both dieter and Lenten faster the exercise of temperance means taking in less food. At the same time, one could agree that *"formaliter"* the acts differ specifically from one another for the reasons stated above. On the surface, at least, this distinction would mean that, although the loss of life for both martyr and soldier of fortune amounts to the same physical action, namely, death, the formal measure of the martyr's strength—in effect, the fortitude of Christ—differs specifically from whatever factors motivate a soldier of fortune to risk life-threatening circumstances.[39] The following text develops this point:

> Although the act of an acquired and an infused virtue remain identical when looked at from the point of view of the physical action itself, still they are not when considered from the point of view of their actual forms. For acquired virtue determines the particulars of a moral action so as to render it proportionate to the good of society. Infused virtue, on the other hand, seeks [to supply human actions with] a proportion ordered towards the good of eternal life. Thus, something judged excessive by one standard could actually become virtuous according to another standard. Take, for example, the case of the one who fasts and even willingly risks death on account of the defense of the faith.[40]

Aquinas seeks to emphasize that the particular shape or "form" which the infused virtues give to one who lives by faith amounts to more than just a new motive.

The new "form" which the infused virtue puts in the believer amounts to a real participation in the *imitatio Christi*. If we consider some of the distinctive features of New Testament morality, it becomes clear that this formal difference entails a radical change of life. We read that the life of faith explains the summons to a self-renunciation that goes to the extreme of martyrdom (Mk 8:35 *passim*), the command to love one's enemies (Mt 5:43–47), to renounce one's rights (e.g., 1 Cor 6:1–8), and not to countenance divorce (Mk 10:2–12; 1 Cor 7:10f). The infused virtues also facilitate and color the characteristic Christian relationship to the world, a relationship both distanced and involved (1 Cor 7:29ff.), and calls for voluntary self-denial and poverty (2 Cor 6:4–10), separation from family[41] (Lk 14:26), and celibacy (Mt 19:12; 1 Cor 7).[42] The Christian, then, possesses the same disposition towards the Heavenly Father and his rule that Christ himself manifests throughout his life.

As every Christian should appreciate, such activities require not only a new set of divinely revealed norms, but also the capacity to follow them.[43] The perfection of Christ's own virtues provides us with a key to interpret what formal difference the infused virtues make in one who is united to Christ. In his discussion of Christ's grace, Aquinas poses the question of whether Christ actually possessed all of the virtues, and replies: "Since grace was at its very best in Christ, it gave rise to virtues which perfected each of the faculties of the soul and all its activities."[44] In the same text, Aquinas responds to the objection that one could not count temperance and continence among the virtues of Christ, who, being without disordered passions, could have no use for such dispositions. Aquinas affirms that Christ possessed not even the beginning of disordered passion,[45] but he also explains how Christ could possess the virtue of temperance:

> Indeed, the more one remains free from base desires the more perfectly temperate is he. And this is why Aristotle puts the

difference between a temperate man and a continent man in the fact that the one does not experience the base desires which trouble the other. Taking continence in the sense that Aristotle did, the very fact that Christ had all the virtues means that he did not have continence. For continence remains something less than virtue.[46]

The formal difference which distinguishes infused from acquired virtue means that the Christian believer enjoys the freedom which the Gospel promises. What is more important, this new excellence of character derives from the personal dignity of Christ himself.

VIRTUES OF PERSONAL DISCIPLINE

Theologians usually distinguish the moral virtues into two categories: the virtues of personal discipline (*circa passiones*) and the virtues associated with justice (*circa operationes*). The virtues of personal discipline include the cardinal virtues of temperance and fortitude along with their allied virtues. In general, these virtues remain ordered towards the indispensable human works of conserving and continuing both the individual person and the human species by facilitating resistance to threatening evils and promoting the pursuit of indispensable goods. The infused virtues of temperance and fortitude advance these same goals within the context of personal union with Christ in the Church of faith and sacraments. "Thus infused temperance," writes Aquinas, "does not have as its final purpose to moderate the concupiscence of touch, rather it does this in imitation of the Kingdom of Heaven."[47]

The formal difference which marks off the infused from the acquired virtues involves reference to the sacrificial character of Christian life. The infused virtues impress the sign of the cross onto the human virtues. Aquinas recognized the efficacy and centrality of Christ's death in establishing the new order of grace, and existentialist theologians rightly point out that the decision to follow Christ repeatedly energizes the moral life of the believer. In this context, decision implies a complete and total choice whereby a person takes up a position, a radical attitude of either acceptance or rejection, with respect to another. In other words, one decides whether or not to become a disciple, willing to follow in all things the person who makes the urgent appeal, "Come, follow me."[48] Discipleship, however, as Bonhoeffer reminds us, costs something. For us sinners the freedom of the children of God often becomes a heavy cross both with regard to our personal decisions and in the framework of community life. The infused virtues enable the believer both to undertake the *imitatio Christi* and to support the share in the sufferings of Christ which it inevitably brings. In particular, infused temperance and fortitude strengthen the believer in those areas of Gospel life which most require that one be conformed to the cross of Christ.

VIRTUES OF JUSTICE AND PRUDENCE

The dynamics which regulate the infused virtues of personal discipline generally hold as well for the virtues *circa operationes*. Justice includes among its principal concerns the actual shaping of the social order.[49] Of course, the transformation of the social order into the Kingdom of God results in that entirely new order which appears in the Christian Church. Indeed, such ecclesiological reasons urge moral realists to argue that infused justice operates differently from the infused virtues of personal discipline. Because infused justice possesses as its distinctive concern the well-being of the Christian community, that is, the Church, the end result of its practice involves the realization of the Body of Christ on earth. So Aquinas contends that even the "physical" stuff with which infused justice deals undergoes a kind of transformation which renders it different from the created stuff of political justice. In other terms, the infused virtues of justice differ also "*materialiter*" from the acquired, "political" virtues of justice.

This astonishing thesis, mainly developed by the Thomist commentatorial tradition, unquestionably evokes some solid and specific eschatological convictions. Aquinas even advanced the opinion that the infused cardinal virtues continue to play an active role even in the life of beatitude. Realist moral theology maintains distinct views on the continuity between the Church on earth and the heavenly Church *in patria*. "Now one is not only a citizen of an earthly state, but [the believer] is also a citizen of the heavenly Jerusalem, where the Lord rules, where the angels and all the saints are the citizens, whether they reign in glory and are at rest in their true country, or whether they are as yet pilgrims on this earth."[50] The infused virtue of justice contributes to the realization of eschatological fulfillment. Biblical theologians, albeit in a different fashion, stress the same point when they point out how similar expectations influenced the moral outlook of the early Church.[51] Jesus instructs us that even a cup of cold water given to someone "because he is a disciple" merits the reward of everlasting life (Mt 10:42). Accordingly, this special feature of infused virtues indicates the essential part which justice plays in a realized eschatology. In his little treatise *De virtutibus cardinalibus*, Aquinas makes a similar point: "Obviously, the acquired virtues, about which the philosophers speak, perfect us only for life in the secular world. They do not, however, ready us for eternal glory."[52]

Prudence affects all of the moral virtues; they cannot function without it. Accordingly, an obvious corollary of the doctrine of the infused virtues is that the infused virtues also require infused prudence. How else could the virtues of personal discipline discover a measure which exceeds that supplied by *recta ratio*? Acquired prudence, dependent solely on the light of human reason, knows nothing about what the *imitatio Christi* entails. This remains the case despite the fact that even natural prudence derives its content from the Eternal Law. Otherwise the radical distinctiveness of Christ's teaching would be rendered either superfluous or a duplication of what already lay available to us through natural inclination and reasoning. Thus, infused personal prudence guides the believer to act, as St. Paul urges, in accord with the mind of Christ. On the other hand, infused political prudence directs those charged with positions of authority in the community. Since infused justice involves deliberation about the up-building or guidance of the Church, this virtue relies on infused political prudence. Otherwise, as in the case of a Christian politician, infused personal prudence suffices to direct the exercise of justice set upon the common good of the *polis*. The distinction is not meant to encourage a double standard, rather it envisions the gradual transformation of the human city according to revealed moral norms.

Like the baroque architecture of the Catholic Reform, Aquinas's conception of the infused virtues manifests the conviction that grace moves everything which transpires in the created order gracefully up into glory: the Kingdom of God on earth. While maintaining this eschatological perspective, the realist moral theologian must continually sound the harmonies between God's action in nature and grace. Still, only the bond of charity guarantees exemplary *communio* in this life and perfect union *in patria;* or, as the poet says, we belong to the Church of Glory!

The infused moral virtues, guided by infused prudence, furnish a specific representation of what such *communio* entails. Also, their realization in the lives of believers really exhibits the true glory which grace makes possible for the Church. In the final analysis, the universal providence of God, extending to all things sweetly and strongly, persuades the theologian of the existence of the infused virtues. In fact, we find a commendable apology for the infused virtues in Aquinas's tract on the grace of the New Law.

We are helped by God's gratuitous will . . . when some habitual grace is infused by God into the soul. And this is because it is not fitting that God should provide less for those whom he loves with a view to their obtaining a supernatural good than for creatures whom he loves with a view to their obtaining a natural good. Now he provides for creatures of nature not only by moving them to natural actions, but also by bestowing on them forms and powers which are the originating principles of actions, so that of themselves they tend to movements of this kind. Thus the movements by which they are moved by God becomes connatural and easy to them, according to the text of Wisdom 7:1, 'She orders all things sweetly.' All the more, then, does he infuse supernatural forms or qualities into those whom he moves towards obtaining an eternal, supernatural good, whereby they may be moved by him sweetly and promptly towards obtaining the eternal good.[53]

This explication of the infused virtues demonstrates the power which grace extends to each one who believes in Christ. Now let us consider the significant advantages which the position holds for some of the important issues which face contemporary moral theology.

DYNAMICS OF INFUSED VIRTUES

In light of the distinction between the infused and acquired virtues, we can envisage two concrete alternatives: first, the case of the believer, who enjoys the life of grace but does not possess a particular acquired virtue; second, the case of the person who possesses acquired virtue, but, for whatever reason, does not enjoy the benefits of a living relationship with Christ. The moral life unfolds differently in each case. Consider the status of the newly baptized.

Juridical categories remain hopelessly inadequate in sacramental theology, which has to deal with community actions whose symbolism is transformed by the intervention of Christ. Theologians teach that the character of baptism places the seal of the risen Christ, imparted by the Spirit, on those who receive it. Although questions about the relationship of grace to the infused virtues exercised authors during the period of high scholasticism, it suffices to observe that baptism gives those who receive it a gift which falls within the logic of the Incarnation, the possibility of joining with Christ in his sacramental worship. When those brought to faith by the preaching of the Word receive baptism, they confess their belief publicly as the community of believers welcomes them. Incorporation into Christ means, among other benefits, that those who are baptized possess the ability to live in conformity with the norms established for Christian conduct.[54] This accounts for the common Christian teaching that, at baptism, the believer receives the full complement of the infused virtues. The *Roman Catechism* calls this the "*comitatum gratiae.*" This effect of baptism also recalls the important connection which the Church recognizes between worship and morality.

The case of infant baptism presents a special set of difficulties. What meaning can be assigned to the presence of the infused virtues in one whose psychological consititution is not developed enough to serve as the basis for an acquired *habitus*? The scholastic theologians, whose motto "Always distinguish" served them well, replied that, for the infant, the infused virtues supplied only the principles of virtuous operation. These virtues could not account for the actual practice of virtue, since the individual lacked the physical and psychological abilities required for any moral act. In the case of the infant, then, the actualization of the infused virtues would accompany the normal development of human maturity which results from Christian upbringing. Aquinas even defines fornication as morally defective partially on the basis that one cannot assure that the child of such a union will receive proper supervision.[56] In any event, the theology of the virtues upholds the importance of both Christian instruction and parental guidance for children.

On the other hand, the adult who receives baptism already possesses the developed physical and psychological capacities which make the practice of virtue possible. Since there is no such thing as a purely supernatural human action, the infused virtues, which amount to freely given graces, cannot by themselves account exclusively for any human action, not even one which comes under the influence of divine grace. Still, the infused virtues do establish a capacity—a principle—for salvific actions which result from the believer's incorporation into Christ. Aquinas explains how this "principle" of the infused virtue operates, "Facility of operation with respect to virtuous activity comes about in two ways: first, from a previous *habitus,* but the infused virtues do not supply this kind of facility; second, as an originating principle, which comes about as a result of a strong adherence to the object of virtue. And this [kind of facility] infused virtue bestows immediately, by way of principle."[57] An early Christian document substantially supports this interpretation of baptism's effect on the moral life of the believer. The *Letter to Barnabas* tells us: "This means that we go down into the water full of sins and foulness, and we come up bearing fruit in our hearts, fear and hope in Jesus in the Spirit."[58]

The infused virtues provide believers with a unique moral capacity; for, given the presence of these virtues, the members of Christ adhere strongly to the object of virtue. This means that the newly baptized adult, whatever the actual state of his acquired moral development, possesses a source or principle for right conduct which derives exclusively from baptismal faith. Christ himself now makes it possible for such a one to adhere to the object of virtue. The believer, as a result of baptism's sacramental efficacy, enjoys a personal relationship with Jesus which cannot fail to provide whatever Christian virtue requires.[59] Although current liturgical practice rightly emphasizes pre-baptismal preparation for adults coming to faith, the full effects of incorporation into Christ result only from the action of the Spirit effectively completed in the baptismal bath. By baptismal grace, the believer possesses a source of moral strength previously unavailable: "we come up bearing fruit in our hearts, fear and hope in Jesus in the Spirit." Moreover, this new moral strength belongs both to those who already possess the acquired virtues and to those who approach baptism with vicious *habitus,* but it functions differently in each case.

One can consider two typical cases. The first is the adult who comes to Christian faith and baptism with certain bad *habitus,* specific acquired vices. The complete gratuity of divine grace means that its bestowal never depends on the moral status of the one who receives it. God loves us, not because we are good, but because he is.[60] Thus it remains entirely possible that adults who come to the saving waters of baptism, although they may possess the resolve to renounce Satan and sin, still bear the marks of past sins. Statistically, this undoubtedly is true of the majority of actual cases. In this circumstance, what do the infused virtues accomplish?

As a result of the disordered *habitus,* a tension arises between the absence of the facility for action, which would otherwise be present with acquired virtue, and the strong adherence to virtue's objects *de facto* provided by the infused virtues. One recognizes a resemblance to the Protestant Reform's *simul justus et peccator*—a just one and a sinner at the same time—in this description of what amounts to the ordinary life of the believer. On the other hand, the doctrine of the infused virtues clearly asserts that the perfection of Christian moral life remains open even to the one who experiences the lingering effects of what St. Paul calls the "old self." This happens to the extent that believers, who recognize the power of infused virtue to ensure that disordered passions in no way gain the upper hand in their lives, cling to Christ in faith. Of course, this status assumes a clear comprehension of the difference between the rational appetite and the sense appetites. Since charity and hope unite the members with the Head, one clings to Christ through the rational appetite. This kind of union, moreover, can coexist—think of Christ alone with the apostles in the storm (Mk 4:35–41)—with even the most violent movements of the sense appetites.

Aquinas shows himself consciously influenced by the Pauline teaching on this matter when, using the language of the schools, he seeks to explain the different effects which the acquired and infused virtues produce in the human passions or emotions. He admits that apart from an extraordinary and miraculous grace, such as St. Paul himself sought from God,[61] disordered emotions are not completely suppressed by either acquired or infused virtue. "For the desires of the flesh are against the Spirit," as St. Paul told the Galatians, "and the desires of the Spirit are against the flesh; for these are opposed to each other, to prevent you from doing what you would" (Gal 5:17). Yet both acquired and infused virtues accomplish something towards subduing disordered emotions, but in different ways. Aquinas explains:

> Acquired virtue effects that the attacks of concupiscence be felt less. This effect results from the causality of acquired virtue; by the frequent acts whereby one grows accustomed to virtue, he gradually grows unaccustomed to obey his passions and begins to resist them. From this there ensues that he sense their attacks the less. Infused virtue is of value in that, even though the passions be felt, they still in no way gain control. For infused virtue effects that one in no way obey the concupiscence of sin; and while this virtue remains, it does this infallibly. Acquired virtue falls short in this respect, although in only a few instances, as other natural inclinations fail in only a minor part.[62]

This confidence in the power of grace surely reflects the New Testament's assurance to believers that God's grace will not fail them under any circumstances. "And he [Christ] awoke and rebuked the wind, and said to the sea, 'Peace! Be still!' And the wind ceased, and there was a great calm. He said to them, 'Why are you afraid? Have you no faith?' And they were filled with awe, and said to one another, 'Who then is this, that even wind and sea obey him?'" (Mk 4:39–41).

Such radical union of the believer with Christ forms the basis of all authentic Christian morality, but it remains open only to those willing to live by faith. No empirical theory can explain how confidence in the power of the blood of Christ in our lives opens up the possibility for fulfilling the requirements of Christian virtue. Theologians who defend the compromise of certain virtues, especially chastity and purity, on the basis that specific individuals remain psychologically ill-disposed to live in accord with their moral requirements, unfortunately ignore a crucial element of Christian moral theology and life. As a result, those who follow the pattern of compromise not only settle for a kind of behavior which leaves the inclinations of human nature unfulfilled, they also miss the opportunity for realizing conformity with Christ. This results in a much larger compromise of Christian doctrine than that which occurs as the result of some immoral practice.

To remain united with Christ means to share in the sufferings of Christ. Aquinas asserts that infused virtue does not at once always remove the sting of disordered emotional attraction or repulsion; its operation does not all at once bring about delight, especially in the early stages of living by faith. Still, the definition of infused virtue as an authentic *habitus* holds, since, as Aquinas explains, "at times it is sufficient for virtue that it work without sadness."[63] An accurate appropriation of the implications of this truth would provide great help to those whose emotional states discourage them from seeking further instruction in Christian life. This truth also recalls that authentic Christian virtue can exist in those whose impulses and urges might otherwise lead them to despair of a closer relationship with Christ and his Church. St. Cyprian affirmed that Christ gives strength to believers in proportion to the trust that each man or woman who receives that strength is willing to place in him.[64]

The second case which the distinction between the acquired and the infused virtues requires us to consider concerns the person who approaches baptism with good *habitus* already acquired. Christian realism rejects the heterodox view which holds that any apparently good act accomplished outside immediate contact with the Christian dispensation amounts to a "splendid vice." And although it is true that the complete perfection of even natural activities, at least when seen as a composite of behavior ordered towards human flourishing, requires that one possess theological charity, still Aquinas found no difficulty in accepting that one could develop some authentic virtue without special divine assistance.[65]

As the custom of presenting the commandments to those petitioning for baptism well before the actual sacrament attests, the ordinary practice of the Christian Church supposes that individuals approach baptism already disposed towards living a large part of the Christian moral life. Incorporation into Christ in such cases means the infused virtues discover the requisite psychological structure for their operation. Obviously such a situation does not render union with Christ nugatory. For the acquired *habitus* permits the newly baptized, now rendered capable of meritorious acts as a result of incorporation into the death and resurrection of Christ, to live out the virtues within the Church. In this context, as the notion of merit implies, Christians actively cooperate in the direction of their whole moral lives, now directed towards supernatural beatitude. Since no merit exists without grace, the act of acquired virtue cannot be meritorious except through the corresponding infused virtue.[66]

The merit of Christ and its efficient role in the lives of believers remain topics foreign to much of contemporary Christology. Concern for discovering the historical dimensions of Christ's human personality evidently deters some theologians from asking what significance the humanity of Christ holds for his properly salvific mission. Aquinas approached the matter from a different perspective. He never tired of repeating that Christ, precisely as a human being, could spiritually influence other men and women and that his works could also cause worthiness for achieving glory in others. Accordingly, classical theology affirms that Christ merited with full worthiness for others—what is called *"ex condigno"* or condign merit. This happens only because Christ, whose humanity was the instrument of his divinity, possesses the ability to exercise a real causality on those who belong to his Body the Church.[67] Indeed, one explains this effect only by appeal to the distinctively Christian dogma concerning the divinity of Christ.

In like manner, baptism constitutes the first sacramental moment when this instrumentality begins to affect those who, led by the Holy Spirit, confess the essentials of Christian belief. Although God never binds himself to any created reality, even a sacrament, still the seven sacraments remain the principal means for taking part in the Christian mysteries. In the living out of that mystery, the infused virtues maintain their importance as Christ's gifts to his members. They remain the only effective means whereby the unity for which Christ repeatedly asks his Heavenly Father comes about in the Church. There brothers and sisters, under the continuous movement of the Holy Spirit, can love one another in accord with God's plan for human fulfillment and for the perfection of the divine glory (Jn 15:8–11).

The sacrament of reconciliation provides another moment when the efficacy of Christ's instrumentality, effected now by sorrow for sin expressed in the presence of the absolving priest, enables a post-baptismal sinner to regain infused virtue. Whether the adult finds Christ in the sacrament of baptism or the sacrament of penance matters little as far as the spiritual dynamics of the acquired and infused virtues go. St. Ambrose recognized the basic unity behind the sacramental system. "If baptism is certainly the remission of all sins, what difference does it make whether priests claim that this power is given to them in penance or at the font? In each the mystery is one."[68] Admittedly, the practice of frequent confession, encouraged by the Church, requires that the faithful receive good instruction about the effects of the sacrament of reconciliation. Otherwise the doctrine of the infused virtues, intended to promote the practice of Christian virtue, could appear an easy escape from the responsibility of actively undertaking a full measure of Christian discipline.

Christian spirituality should find the doctrine of the infused virtues indispensable for authentic development in the life of faith. The full complement of infused virtues allows no room for the Quietist tendency, which depreciates the role of human effort and creativity, to interpret the whole of Christian existence as a single expression of undifferentiated "pure love."[69] Rather, divine grace penetrates human nature and, as the adage says, perfects it. Western theology struggles to maintain and interpret the richly suggestive intuition of the Greek Fathers that the very union of God with human nature brought redemption to all that is human.[70] The theology of the infused moral virtues represents the best effort of the medieval theologians, especially Aquinas, to apply that intuition to matters of moral theology. Faith, hope, and charity imprint their own divine mark on human activity. But the theology of the infused moral virtues ensures that in setting forth the Christian doctrine on divinization moral theology loses nothing authentically human.

6. CHARACTERISTICS OF THE VIRTUES

DISTINCTIVENESS OF CHRISTIAN TEACHING

The Fathers of the Church liked to stress that grace appears not only in the saints' words, but also on their faces. This is as much to say that the moral virtues effect recognizable changes in every aspect of a person's life. Those moral theologians who wrote about virtue usually considered certain related questions as part of their standard exposition, with three in particular receiving attention: first, whether virtue observes a mean; second, whether the virtues are connected; and, third, whether all the virtues exist more or less equally in a given individual. While common experience might induce us to hesitate in the face of these queries, especially those concerning the connection and equality of the moral virtues,[1] both pagan philosophers and Christian moralists alike have traditionally taught that the moral virtues observe a mean and are concatenate. This final chapter introduces these corollaries to a theology of the moral virtues.

New Testament teaching on the power of Christ in the moral life compels theologians to explore the characteristics of virtue. St. Paul reminded his converts in Galatia of the integrity of life which Christian life demands. Apparently, certain recidivist members of the community had returned to practices inconsistent with Paul's preaching on the moral and theological unity of Gospel faith. "Are you so foolish?"

he chided them. "Having begun with the Spirit, are you now ending with the flesh?" (Gal 3:3). Thus, as other examples from the Pauline writings make clear, consistent moral practice in the individual and in the community remains an essential feature of the Christian dispensation. So much is this the case that the Letter to the Ephesians can insist that Christ died so that he "might present the church to himself in splendor, without spot or wrinkle or any such thing, that she might be holy and without blemish" (Eph 5:25–27).[2]

But how does this assertion square with the notion of a pilgrim Church and with the thesis that even the infused virtues leave our emotions frayed? Dominic Bañez, formidable opponent of Molinism[3] and trusted confidant of St. Teresa, offered this realistic but encouraging appraisal of what the believer can expect divine charity to accomplish in the moral life:

> That difficulty which the just one, i.e., who lives in divine charity, experiences in his operations, arises from the passions, which are not directly and formally opposed to charity. Thus, even when perfect charity is immediately infused into the repentant sinner, who is strengthened by sincere contrition, the sensitive appetites are not, as a result, quelled. Still, there remains in the justified one the power of moderating those rebellious emotions.[4]

Bañez, who established the principles for spiritual direction in the golden epoch of Spanish mysticism, points out how divine charity forms the basis for an even life of virtue. This effect of grace can happen as well in one whose emotional life remains marked by the lingering effects of bad behavior.

Accordingly, the moral theologian can take a sanguine approach to the question of how the virtues work, both in themselves and along with one another. Christian theology understands that divine grace strengthens everyone who lives by faith, whereas philosophy can only assume such excellence in the best of women and men. St. Paul likewise affirms that it is Christ himself who unites faith and practice in the believer. So he pleads with the Galatians: "My little children, with whom I am again in travail until Christ be formed in you!" (Gal 4:19). This faith assertion about the role of Christ in the moral life (which merits the attention of contemporary students of spirituality and counseling) forms the nucleus of Pauline teaching on the Christian life. Those who live without an active faith in Christ must imagine that the characteristics of the virtuous life, such as their unity and equality, represent only a paragon of virtue. Like any ideal, the virtuous life could not be achieved except by a stouthearted few.

Since theology remains a divine science, a *sacra doctrina,* the theologian must weigh the implications of a philosophical doctrine once it has been put at the service of Christian revelation. The moral theologian must interpret the properties of virtue which moral philosophers propose according to a specifically theological hermeneutic. Recall that the classic authors on the spiritual life stressed that grace affects every part of human nature, not just its "spiritual" element. (The saints expressed Christ on their faces.) But even the most optimistic appraisal of what grace can accomplish proves difficult to reconcile with Gregory the Great's blunt assertion: "One virtue without the others amounts to either nothing or defective virtue."[5] At the same time, St. Jerome provides both a precedent and a good example of how to accommodate philosophy for theological purposes: "To be sure, the opinion of philosophers holds that virtue is a mean, rejecting vice's outlandishness. But it's difficult to hold on to a mean in everything. So for us, a simple phrase suffices: 'Let us commit nothing excessive!'"[6]

THE MEAN OF VIRTUE

Philosophical teaching about virtue as the embodiment of moderation made an impression on the earliest Christian moralists. Gregory of Nyssa even refers to it in his mystical *Commentary on the Song of Songs*.[7] Aristotle insisted that observing a mean amounted to the very essence of virtue, "Virtue is a state that decides, [consisting] in a mean, the mean relative to us, which is defined by reference to reason, i.e., to the reason by reference to which the intelligent person would define it."[8] This definition, which betrays the moral elitism generally characteristic of philosophical ethics, nonetheless influenced the medieval schoolmen. But to define virtue as observing a rational mean, determined by the wise of this world, poses difficulties for the theologian. Such an approach seems uncongenial to a basic New Testament intuition which, in various ways, sets up the childlike as the standard norm for Christian wisdom. Any number of texts make the point that the Kingdom of Heaven belongs to those who remain little in the eyes of the world (Mt 18:1–4; Mk 9:33–37; Lk 9:46–48). Our near-contemporary saint, Thérèse of Lisieux, retrieved this scriptural vision for the twentieth century in her doctrine on the "Little Way" of spiritual childhood.[9]

The New Testament also obliges us to recall that Christ continually presents himself as a friend of sinners. The preeminent example is Mary Magdalene. The philosophers would say that she lacked the virtue of chastity, the virtue in the concupiscible appetite which avoids both the extremes of insensibility and unmeasured indulgence. But Jesus showed Mary Magdalene that her sin was in not loving enough, that she sought in human love what only God's love could give her. In other words, Jesus refuses to condemn the sinner for failure to observe the mean of virtue. To be sure, Mary Magdalene was a sinner by Christian standards, namely, she had made an idol out of created love in the measure that her appetite was instinctively motivated, but while the philosophical motive shows what evil is and where virtue lies, it is Christ who shows us how to become truly virtuous. This happens when we give ourselves to him as we are; not by trying to impose a rational measure on our appetites, but by the realization that all the extremes of our desires find their fulfillment in him.

Right reason, *recta ratio,* cannot develop in a mind turned in on itself; for practical intelligence formed by prudence, only discovers its proper directions in the Eternal Law. Even the first stirrings of *synderesis* reflect the godly image.[10] Accordingly, Christian moral realism can not follow certain philosophers of the modern period, such as Hobbes and Kant, who depreciate the virtuous mean; these secular moralists concluded that observance of a mean implies moral mediocrity, not excellence.[11] The mean of virtue which prudence establishes does not settle for some hypothetical middle ground between the morally good and bad. Rather, right reason sets its imprint on the emotions and other operations, so that one avoids the extremes of excess and defect in moral matters. Since prudence infallibly conforms a particular choice to right reason, the virtuous mean requires no further clarification, such as a theory of "commensurate reasons,"[12] to achieve the optimum of moral excellence.

THE MORAL VIRTUES

The mean of virtue averts two different defective moral forms, i.e., two opposed forms of evil: excess and defect. Theological ethics applies a further distinction to the moral virtues, *viz.,* between a real mean and the reasoned mean. The virtues of operation, justice and its allied virtues, observe an objective or real mean, one equated with the particular "thing" or object which determines these virtues' measure. But the virtues of the emotions, fortitude and temperance along with their allied virtues, observe a reasoned mean, one established on the basis of subjective factors, such as an individual's particular strengths and capacities. In both cases, however, prudence directs virtue towards achieving the correct mean.

In the case of a reasoned mean, prudence weighs two factors indispensable for the correct development of virtue in the sense appetites. The first is a material factor, the biological stuff, if you will, out of which the virtue emerges. In the case of temperance, this amouts to the strong delectations and attractions required for health and reproduction; in the case of fortitude, an instinctive aversion to what is corruptive, or a strong sense of securtiy. Next, since the conditions in which particular emotions act must also be taken into account, the actual circumstances of a virtuous act also figure in assessing the reasoned mean. This second factor can include as many different people, events, and things as one might encounter in the course of a lifetime. Some examples will better illustrate the point.

First, we consider the reasoned mean and sins of excess. Here, the reasoned mean establishes a virtuous norm of restraint for the material element of virtue. Otherwise, when the emotions operate without regulation, they can force one beyond the correct mean, so that sinful excess occurs. For example, the person who piles up a surplus of material goods when the Church calls for restraint in consumer-oriented societies exceeds what virtuous passion permits as regards personal belongings. Or, to take another case, the one who achieves sexual gratification outside the commitment which Christian marriage requires veers from the rational mean for venereal pleasures. Again, excess is present when a soldier precipitously enters a dangerous battle assignment without proper preparations or when a person of average income seeks to accomplish tasks that require the expenditures of large sums of money. In each of these cases, we see instances where a person's emotions push them to some form of self-indulgence. Accordingly, such people fall short in the virtues of personal discipline; in the examples given, modesty, purity, courage, and magnificence respectively.

Secondly, the reasoned mean also avoids sinful defect. This occurs when one fails to summon up the amount of emotional energy required to realize virtue. Different moral situations require a range of emotional responses, even very strong ones. When prudence dictates that a certain level of emotional energy is appropriate to achieve the correct mean, deficient passion can destroy the reasoned mean as much as excessive emotion does. For example, if someone succumbs to anxiety when confronted with an onerous situation or remains insensitive to the legitimate, even sexual, needs of a marriage partner, such behavior can fall short of what virtue requires in these existential circumstances. Likewise, immobilizing fear at a time when one should stand up for some good cause, or restraining inhibitions when one should take the initiative in personal relations result from defects of the irascible appetites. In these cases, sinful defect occurs because one has not exercised the requisite emotion for patience, conjugal chastity, fortitude, and meekness respectively. The reasoned mean, then, determines what course virtuous activity should take for each individual in consideration of the contingencies thrown up by a multiplicity of diverse moral situations.

In the case of the real mean (after the Latin, *medium rei*), prudence takes into account still another sort of moral condition. Justice finds its mean in the particular thing (*res*) involved in exchange, as this relates to those "rights" (*jus*) which establish the foundation for relations between individuals and communities. So, for example, the proprietors of a firm owe a just wage—the mean of justice—to their employees, as this is determined by the requirements of economic justice and, consequently, stipulated in a legal contract. The virtue of justice institutes the real mean in two different ways. In the case of commutative justice, which governs exchanges, there exists an arithmetical equality which determines whether a particular action achieves its just measure. For example, one cannot ordinarily make restitution for $500.00 worth of damages with $50.00, or for detraction against one's neighbor with anything short of the whole truth. However, in the case of distributive justice, which governs the relationship of a community to its members, or general justice, which looks after the duties of individuals to the common good, a geometrical equality obtains. In such cases, the virtuous mean amounts to a proportion established in consideration of a number of pertinent factors. Graduated income tax provides the obvious example of this real mean in the case of general justice; social security payments and Medicare represent the real mean in distributive justice.

All of the virtues allied with justice, such as the virtues of veneration and civility, operate according to a real mean. The virtues of veneration, religion, piety, and respect, establish an objective mean as regards our obligations towards God, towards parents and homeland, and towards legitimate authority, respectively. The virtues of civility, such as gratitude, friendship, and liberality, also entail a real mean, though admittedly the adventitious character of these virtues makes reckoning it more difficult than for distributive and commutative justice.

Finally, social justice falls into a special category.[13] Since this hybrid virtue results from a composite of various forms of the cardinal virtue of justice, it is sometimes difficult to agree on what constitutes social justice's legitimate mean. Although philosophers analyze legal or general justice, there is something specifically Christian about social justice. The Church places Gospel values first among the oftentimes competing factors which figure in social issues. Similarly, humility and poverty remain distinctively Christian virtues, not because others cannot practice or write about them, but because few moralists appraise them according to biblical standards. Thus, the gift of counsel manifests itself principally in the leadership of the Church, so as to determine the prudent and evangelical course for the community. As a result, to discover the real mean of social justice requires careful attention to the givens of Christian revelation and the ecclesiastical Magisterium. Otherwise, the infused virtue could easily collapse into one or another variant of political ideology, instead of embodying a constitutive element of New Testament morality.

Since justice observes a real mean in establishing the just due for any circumstance, there exists only one possibility for deviation, namely, sinful defect. Unlike the virtues of personal discipline, where each virtue has its form of sinful excess and defect, a single vice, namely, injustice, stands opposed to justice. Indeed, to give more than what is required constitutes a virtue, not a vice (on the supposition, of course, that one is not neglecting other duties by giving more). On the other hand, to suffer injustice, as Aquinas explains in his commentary on Aristotle's *Nicomachean Ethics,* can be something virtuous.

> Justice is not a mean in the same way as the other moral virtues. Their mean lies between two extremes, vices; liberality is a mean between parsimony and extravagance. But justice is not a mean between two vices. However, it may be called a mean by reason of its effect in as much as it constitutes a mean, since its act is a just operation which is a mean between doing what is unjust and bearing the unjust. The first of these, active injustice pertains to a vice of injustice which is a habit of extremes in as much as it takes for itself too many goods and too few evils. But the other, namely, the tolerance of the injustice is not a vice, but a suffering.[14]

For the theologian, the passion of Christ situates this philosophical teaching within an entirely new perspective, one in which suffering becomes instrumental for our salvation.

THE "VICIOUS CIRCLE" OF PRUDENCE?

Realist moral theology must also deal with the mean of the intellectual virtues. Of course, realist philosophy considers truth *"per conformitatem ad rem"* as the just mean for the virtues of the speculative intellect. Although this question does not directly affect moral theology, except insofar as speculative truth concerns any theological discipline, it does raise again the question about truth and the practical intellect. Granted aesthetics also interests the ethicist, the mean of prudence requires explicit analysis. For example, John Oesterle admirably summarizes Aquinas's teaching: "In prudence, right reason as establishing the mean is the measure of the movement of appetite; the mean in moral virtues, accordingly, is to be measured by this right reason. Because prudence is an intellectual virtue, right reason is directive in relation to appetite; because moral virtue is in the appetite, it is directed by right reason.[15]

Although there are specific vices which corrupt the virtue of prudence itself, general imprudence results from neglecting the due measure which should exist between right reason and appetite. For example, when one desires recognition from others beyond what one's abilities merit, the defective mean of vainglory constitutes a form of imprudence. Or, if someone without a secondary education were to seek admission to a medical school, the imprudence would result from a failure to recognize that such ambitions are simply out of touch with reality, with the way things actually are. Hence the mean of prudence, a virtue of the practical intellect, like the other intellectual virtues, requires conformity to that which exists outside the mind. Specifically, given the existence of virtuous ends for human nature, imprudence arises when one acts upon a desire which does not conform to such ends.

Take, for example, heterodox views on the purposes of human sexuality. Although the climate of contemporary debate on the subject of homosexuality remains charged with conflicting viewpoints about its origin and meaning, homosexual conduct nevertheless instantiates imprudent behavior, one which lacks conformity with the "built-in teleologies of human nature." Those who pursue carnal gratification with partners of the same sex, whether acting upon strong desire or not, in fact make a false judgment about the erotic pleasure which results from such behavior.

As happens with any sin, the imprudence consists in the false judgment, an intellectual act, about the relationship of specific actions to the purposes or ends of human nature. Thus, Aquinas explains that such acts are "in conflict with the natural pattern of sexuality for the benefit of the species."[16] Of course, for realist moral theology every morally defective action amounts at least to acting against some good of nature. But the designation of certain specific actions as unnatural indicates that, in matters of sexual behavior especially, the disorder of appetite in relation to a natural end manifests itself in a distinctively graphic way, as actions like cunnilingus and sodomy amply illustrate.[17]

Finally, the question whether the intellectual virtues actually observe a mean offers the chance to look at what some authors have proposed be called the "vicious circle" of prudence. Prudence discovers a mean in rectified appetites as they remain conformed with the authentic ends of human nature. But the appetites depend on prudence in order to direct our activities toward those ends. No prudence means no rectified appetites; unrectified appetites destroy prudence. But if moral virtue is determined by an intellectual virtue, as Aristotle said, "defined by reference to reason," how can one even begin to discover the mean of any virtue? Since prudence observes a mean established by the moral virtues, this implies that one can determine the mean of prudence only by reference to some other virtue. And so it could seem that in order to be prudent one needs an endless series of moral virtues. But Aquinas forestalls such a conclusion by pointing out that there "is no need to have an endless succession of virtues, for the measure and rule of intellectual virtue is not some other kind of virtue, but is things themselves.[18]

Of this simple sentence a French author, working out of the classic commentatorial tradition, exclaims: "Précieuse et profonde remarque!"[19] Aquinas, he explains, underscores that moral virtue finds its rule and measure through intelligence: the correct mean develops from conscientious conformity to moral wisdom. But practical wisdom itself discovers its rule and measure in conformity with reality. Of course, by this we understand reality in all of its dimensions. All in all, only a realist moral theology can express such confidence about the relationship of morality to the created order. In effect, abusive use of human capacities bumps up against reality, even if reality does not always respond immediately. It takes time, for example, before a society which does not respect the value of the human word sees what ill effects the consequent breakdown in human communication causes. Again, it may require several years of sinful disorder before the self-centeredness ingredient in auto-erotic behavior fully emerges in an individual's life. But in due course, imprudences make their effect felt both in the person who commits them and, inevitably, in a society which tolerates them.

One rationale for authentic moral teaching in the Church derives from the fact that experience teaches a hard lesson. Too much time spent in learning moral truths can defeat their efficacy. Human experience, since it relies on trial and error, can only slowly attain ethical wisdom. Thus, Aquinas argued that it was right that we should first be left to ourselves under the regime of the Old Law, in order that by falling into sin and becoming conscious of our own weakness, we would recognize our need for grace to live a fully satisfied life.[20] Although the findings of developmental psychology have greatly influenced the way moral theologians evaluate the moral activity of those beginning to practice virtue, especially adolescents, it is important to remember that Christian theology only recognizes disordered experiments in morality as results of God's permissive providence. His wisdom allows them, but they do not reflect his goodness. In other words, sinful conduct at any stage of development can have no positive value in itself. Yet, it remains difficult to reconcile this classic truth with the view, advanced by some theorists, including Christian psychotherapists, that unmoderated expressions of emotion, such as observed in outbursts of unjust anger or auto-erotic behavior, may play a positive role in one's psycho-social development. Since behavior of such a kind always betrays imprudence and the lack of a reasoned mean, it can only lead to the breakdown, not the excellence of human character.

CONNECTION OF THE VIRTUES

The function of prudence in the moral life suggests another important feature of virtue, namely, the connection or unity of the virtues. As early as the time of St. Augustine, Christian theology had already recognized that this teaching of the philosophers had some useful applications in the Christian moral life.[21] In a letter to St. Jerome, the Doctor of Grace wrote: "Surely [the philosophers] do convince us in this case. The person who possesses one virtue, possesses them all, and the one who lacks a single virtue, lacks them all. For prudence cannot be cowardly, nor unjust, nor intemperate, since where any of these qualities actually exist, prudence can not."[22] Yet even Christian philosophers express reservations on this point.[23] Thus, one best illustrates the unity of virtue by reference to Christ's grace working in the life of the believer.

Some claim that theses like those on the connection and equality of the virtues do not square well with the impressions which result from unsystematized experience. Most people are struck by the conflicting moral qualities of those around them, and not, as this argument proposes, by the uniform quality of moral character. Besides, no one wishes to claim that the intellectual virtues appear uniformly in those who possess them. It is enough for one person to learn the principles of astronomy, without having to develop the skills (i.e., *habitus*) of literary criticism, and so forth. Again, some moral qualities, such as magnificence and humility or courage and meekness, especially if they are not properly understood, seem fundamentally irreconcilable traits for one person to possess at the same time.[24] Despite all this, as realist moral theologians insist, the prudential character of the moral life requires that for any specific virtue to function well, all the virtues must function well. Such insistence derives from the New Testament's universal call to holiness. Christ's prayer that his disciples attain that measure of the holiness which belongs properly to God alone does not allow for compromise. Nonetheless, how to account for the connection of the virtues remains open to legitimate theological debate.

The theologians of the twelfth century were by and large convinced that theological charity alone sufficed to explain the connection of the infused moral virtues. Of course, the formal distinctions among charity, grace, the infused virtues, and even the person of the Holy Spirit remained somewhat confused during the early stages of scholasticism. As a result, theologians of that epoch naturally spoke broadly about what charity accomplished in the individual. One of them, Philip the Chancellor, recognized the need to distinguish at least between the charity which makes us love God for himself and the charity which unites all the other virtues. The latter he called "general charity" to distinguish it from the "specific charity" which united the believer to God.[25] Other authors gave additional explanations, but the basic intuition behind the teaching remained the same, namely, the New Testament's call to practice perfect love of God and neighbor. It should be stressed that this evangelical motive to affirm the connection of the virtues in the believer antedates the reception of Aristotelian ethics by the medieval schoolmen, although it was Aristotle's remark about the inseparability of the virtues that later sparked interest in a theoretical account of the psychological requirements for such a condition to exist.[26]

Thus, in reply to the question of whether the moral virtues are connected with each other, we find that Aquinas recognizes both the theological tradition, quoting Gregory the Great and Augustine, as well as the philosophical argument, citing Aristotle's *Ethics*.[27] Aquinas asserts that the connection of the moral virtues results, on the one hand, from the general characteristics of virtue and, on the other hand, from the operation of prudence in directing the moral life. "The virtues, if they are not connected, cannot be perfect," wrote Gregory the Great, "for there is no true prudence without justice, temperance, and fortitude."[28] "Likewise," adds Aquinas, "one cannot have prudence without having the moral virtues since prudence is right reasoning about what is to be done, whose starting point is the end of action, to which we are rightly disposed by the moral virtues."[29] As we have already spoken about the supposed "vicious circle" of prudence, the following discussion considers why one moral virtue needs all the others in order to function harmoniously as it should.

The contention that the virtues must remain connected in order to be perfect raises some immediate misgivings. What about cases where certain virtues simply remain out of reach for individuals who lack what their exercise requires? For example, while one with meager funds can practice liberality, personal finances will determine whether the same individual can virtuously expend large sums as magnificence requires. True enough, replies Aquinas, but "when one becomes adept in practicing liberality in moderate gifts and spending, if he comes into a large sum of money he would acquire the *habitus* of magnificence with little practice."[30] Thus, he seems to suggest that a comparable internal disposition prepares an individual to practice virtue under circumstances previously unmet.

The scholastic theologians actually coined a phrase for this state. A truly virtuous person could be said to possess any virtue "*in praeparatione animae*" even if at a given moment particular legitimate circumstances prevented the person from actually exercising the virtue. Such preparedness of soul would easily supply the new *habitus* when changed circumstances of life required the heretofore unpracticed virtue. Theologians even assert that virtuous Christian spouses possess the virtue of virginity *"in prae-paratione animae"* so that, in the event of the death of one of them, the practice of celibate chastity would not amount to a burden. Such a confidence in the transforming power of divine grace can also explain how authentic conjugal chastity readies a Christian man and wife to remain united in one flesh, as their marriage covenant requires, without recourse to artificial means for the regulation of conception. The virtues of the married life, which include more than those concerned with the moderation of sexual pleasure, also transform periodic abstinence into a real expression of married love and conjugal communication. The spouses, when circumstances require it, would possess virginity *in praeparatione animae,* so that they might protect and foster the human goods associated with marriage and family life.

However, such explicit claims about the unity of the virtuous life require that certain important qualifications be borne in mind. For example, the connection of the virtues holds only in the case of a *fully developed virtue.* Only "perfect virtue," as Gregory the Great called it, exhibits all the characteristics of a fully formed *habitus.* Accordingly, the life of virtue must attain a certain level of development or completeness in order for connectedness to result. This perfection must occur both in the virtue's own essence or nature and in its actual condition in the one who possesses it. The perfection of a virtue's nature means that the particular virtue includes everything its definition requires and the perfection of condition means that it exists in a given person as a true *habitus.*[31] Thus, a simple disposition—for example, the occasional inclination to observe personal chastity—even if a more or less permanent feature of someone's character, will not mean that one possesses all other virtues. Such imperfect dispositions probably explain the inconsistencies some people cite to discredit the thesis on the unity of the virtues. But "perfect virtue" requires both completeness in itself and firmness in its possessor.

Some examples will serve to illustrate this point. Take the woman who ordinarily possesses a generally calm disposition, but under certain predictable, although exceptional, circumstances becomes and remains very angry. Since her *sang froid* does not extend to every circumstance which requires it, she does not possess the nature of *perfect* meekness. Thus, one would not look for a connection between meekness and the other virtues in her. In the same way, the man who usually treats others only as their merits deserve but occasionally surprises everyone by an extraordinary act of generosity, does not possess the *perfect* condition of liberality. Although in this case the nature of his liberality is complete insofar as he gives beyond the required measure, the pattern is ephemeral and episodic. In the first case, the woman possesses a simple disposition, which resembles a *habitus*; but there are certain objects to which her "virtue" does not extend. So, although she has an habitual grasp on her serenity, still the disposition, given the right provocation, can and does change easily. In the second case, the man also possesses a simple disposition; he does not have a firm hold on the virtue of liberality. As a result, his inclination to act accordingly comes and goes. Since so much unregulated appetite still exists in people with mere dispositions towards a virtuous life, prudence is inhibited from exercising a full measure of direction in the moral life. Consequently, no connection of the virtues can exist, because the property of connectedness requires that the virtues exist in their "perfect" state, namely as a "*habitus* of inclining one to do a good act well."[32]

In sum, "perfect virtue" must actually exist in the subject as a real *habitus,* firmly established in the person's psychology so that a sudden shift in circumstances does not abruptly produce a disinclination to do a good act. It is not enough, for example, for a person to be temperate with wine, but not with cocaine. It is not enough to be chaste at home in the company of one's spouse, but not when called away unexpectedly on a business trip. Only when these two conditions—complete in nature and firm in condition—are met, does a person experience the unity of the virtues.

It is important to recognize that fully developed or "perfect" virtue does not necessarily imply the kind of heroic virtue practiced by the saints. Rather, it consists in a principle of self-assurance which infallibly directs an individual towards the achievement of moral good. Virtue provides those who possess it with this kind of assurance, namely, that they possess whatever the morally good life may require of them, even if until now the opportunity to face a particular situation has not occurred. The principle for this kind of self-assurance lies in prudence, which can steady life according to the single pattern of moral truth, even though the variety of moral goods to be achieved require many different moral virtues.[33] So prudence provides the principal guarantee that an individual life will demonstrate the unity of the virtues. What can prohibit an individual, especially where liberal democracy proclaims the absolute right of each one to do so, from conscientiously making moral choices according to diverse, and even contradictory standards? The answer is prudence, which embodies a single moral wisdom, but adapts it to a variety of personal circumstances. Only after prudence has established moral truth in a person or in a community can the exercise of individual and political liberties achieve both authentic freedom and a just society.

The connection of the virtues, then, actually represents a commonsense truth. Human life is connected. No single virtue, or even a cluster of virtues, can survive in isolation from the others required for human existence. For example, alcoholic beverages jeopardize sobriety, the virtue which moderates the use of intoxicating substances, but so also do objects which belong properly to other virtues, for example, threatening situations. Fortitude or one of its allied virtues braces a person to act well in arduous circumstances. When, therefore, one who lacks fortitude encounters a difficult situation, not only does the vice of cowardice appear, but other virtues are also at risk, as in the common experience that the loss of sobriety frequently results from an individual's inability to face trying situations. At the same time, the unity of the virtues helps us to appreciate the response of those who heard Christ's exchange with the rich ruler. "Then who can be saved?" someone asked; and Jesus replied: "What is impossible with men, is possible with God" (Lk 18:26,27). The doctrine of the connection of the moral virtues makes practical sense only when we consider the transformation divine grace accomplishes in the person of the believer.

Philosophy, as such, knows nothing about supernatural beatitude.[34] Thus, even if it be true, as some contend, that Christianity adds no new virtue to the list drawn up by philosophers, the Christian dispensation discloses a virtuous perfection which only God can bestow and which leads to his kingdom and glory.[35] Commenting on the patristic maxim that charity serves as mother of the virtues, Aquinas avers: "Charity is called the end of the other [moral] virtues because it directs them all to its own end. And since a mother is one who conceives in herself from another, charity is called the mother of the virtues, because from desire of the ultimate end it conceives their acts by charging them with life."[36] At the same time, Aquinas saw no difficulty in affirming that one could develop a complete virtue (philosophically speaking, that is: perfect in its nature and condition, as the genus of virtue requires) without the special divine help of grace.[37] Even so, he would not admit that the practice of such a "perfect" virtue actually drew a person closer to God. Like fine china, moreover, philosophy's virtues are fragile ones.

All things considered, then, only the divine perfection which charity effects in a person ensures that human prudence functions well throughout a whole lifetime. "For when a man does not have his heart firmly established in God," Aquinas writes, "in such a way that he does not wish to be separated from him for the sake of obtaining any good or avoiding any evil, many things arise to obtain or to avoid which man departs from God, rejecting his precepts, and so sins mortally.[38] Grace makes the unity of the virtues a possibility for every believer. What the philosophers took as a description of a distinctive few, a moral oligarchy, the Gospel message proposes for all those who, in faith, accept the power of the risen Christ in their lives. According to Christ's own account, the moral hero of the New Testament remains the one whose basic disposition towards virtue resembles that of a little child. This resemblance manifests itself particularly in something characteristic of the properly loved child, namely, the trait which knows how to receive good things from a parent. One so disposed, therefore, remains psychologically and spiritually inclined to receive from the heavenly Father everything required for a happy and complete life.

And what of those who do not remain, *de facto,* united with Christ? Prudence, unfortified by grace, eventually turns to counterfeit prudence, which makes reason intent on a goal that only seems good. Even if they purport to practice Christian virtue, those who do not live according to the basic truths of the Christian life, remain like branches cut off from the vine.[39] What else can explain the many simulacra of Christian morality? Consider the message of economic and personal self-reliance preached by certain religious sects. To be sure, those who pursue such goals can, and sometimes even do, develop certain "virtues" required for the successful undertaking of bourgeois life, such as gratitude, courage, and sobriety. But Christian social justice, which forms a constitutive part of New Testament morality, sets limits, for example, to the extent unregulated free enterprise can dominate a country's economic resources, nor does the New Testament permit a callous attitude towards the disadvantaged, no matter how much their own lack of personal initiative may account for their state of need. Yet, typically, these unvarnished attitudes coexist even with other virtuous dispositions in the one whose life has not been rooted in Christ.

EQUALITY OF THE VIRTUES

Along with the doctrine on the connection of the virtues and for many of the same reasons, moral realism argues that the virtues develop equally, though according to a certain proportion, in a given person. The virtuous person uniformly practices virtue, not only in possessing all of the virtues, but also in possessing each one equally. As with the other characteristics of virtue, classical moral philosophy first advanced the thesis on the equality of the virtues. The Christian tradition, however, did not hesitate to affirm that whatever claims philosophy could make about human nature,would apply *a fortiori* to those who by faith received a new nature in baptism. So St. Augustine writes: "Those who are equal in fortitude are equal in prudence, justice, and temperance.[40]

Abstractly considered, the virtues are not equal; rather, among themselves they rank according to their capacity to participate in the specifically human power of intelligence. Accordingly, the traditional order of listing the cardinal virtues actually represents their hierarchical structure: prudence, justice, fortitude, and temperance. In addition, the Thomist tradition generally holds that, since their object remains truth itself, the intellectual virtues, again abstractly considered, rank above the moral virtues. Unlike the virtues of the speculative intellect which aspire to truth itself, each of the moral virtues perfects a single psychological power, and can pursue, therefore, only a limited share of good, not goodness itself. This point of view, however, does not gainsay a more primary truth: that only the moral virtues perfect the whole person without qualification. Accordingly, other legitimate schools of Christian theology, which judge that possessing love of the truth is more important than possessing the truth about love, give priority even in the abstract, to the virtues of the rational appetite. But the thesis on the equality of the virtues does not consider virtue in the abstract, but concretely, i.e., as it exists in a given individual.

This does not mean that the moral virtues are the same in everyone. Obviously, just as there are those people who know more than others about one field of theoretical inquiry or another, so also there are those who exercise prudence, justice, fortitude, or temperance more than others do. Common experience confirms this. Besides, if this were not the case, the Church could hold out no motivation for growth in virtue by setting before us the example of the saints, who differ from one another as star differs from star. Virtue requires equality when it is a matter of the objects or situations which it embraces, but allows for inequality when it is a matter of comparing the state of virtue among different persons.

To assert that the moral virtues exhibit equality in any given individual requires a further precision. For while the moral virtues when considered under their formal aspect manifest equality, they can vary under their material aspect. The material aspect of the moral virtues refers to the natural endowments which a given individual possesses. Biology, not morality, accounts for these. One who possesses the physical strength to face up to threatening evils ordinarily develops fortitude with greater ease than one who does not. Again, certain natural dispositions cause some people to experience ease in showing affection, while in others certain traits favor their ability to show restraint. Thus, nature itself renders some people better suited for one virtue than for another. Certain philosophers also emphasize that social forces can play a role in disposing people for one virtue or another.

But if one considers the formal aspect of virtue, that is, the way in which prudence directs the virtuous life,then theological ethics can speak about the equality of the virtues. [41] The unitive function of prudence ensures that the moral virtues demonstrate not only unity but also equality. Since theoreticians, such as Aquinas, offer an explanation for the equality of the virtues similar to that which they give for their interconnectedness, the thesis actually amounts to a corollary of one which affirms the connection of the virtues. In short, since the moral virtues exist together as a unity, they also must maintain, as an ensemble, what in practice amounts to a proportional equality. In fact, Aquinas uses the image of a human hand to make the point. Speaking about the way virtue increases or diminishes in a given individual, he says, "all the virtues of a man or woman are equal proportionally inasmuch as they increase equally in them; in this respect they are like the fingers of a hand which are quantitatively unequal but equal proportionally in that they grow in proportion to one another."[42] Were this not the case, the radical underdevelopment of one virtue would cause a comparable damaging effect on the ensemble of virtues as if the same virtue were altogether absent.

To sum up, the mean, connection, and equality of the virtues give systematic expression to basic theological truths about the moral life. The moral teaching of the New Testament obliges theological ethics to interpret in specific ways the injunction which Jesus gives to his disciples apropos the holiness of the heavenly Father. "You, therefore, must be perfect, as your heavenly Father is perfect" (Mt 5:48). Thereupon, the Christian moral tradition has continually emphasized the beatitudes as principal constituents of the New Law of grace.[43] When moral theologians set forth characteristic qualities of the virtuous life, they attempt to explain coherently how a radical life of Gospel perfection, such as Jesus sets forth in the Sermon on the

Mount, develops in the lives of those whom God calls to share in the image of his Son.

Thus, theological ethics must maintain that the moral virtues are indivisible. For example, in order for justice to exist as a virtue, it must cover every potentially just object and situation. One could not recognize genuine justice in one who stood ready to pay his or her legitimate debts, but who was unwilling to respect the life of an unborn child. Likewise, there can be no such thing as being piecemeal temperate or partially brave when speaking about virtue's extension. Either one possesses long-suffering in every circumstance which requires it, or one cannot be said to be long-suffering. Again, either one amuses oneself properly, or one does not possess perfect eutrapelia, the virtue of recreation and funmaking. Christian perfection does not allow for "easy" virtue, so a true or "perfect" moral virtue always requires its undivided form. Likewise, one cannot choose to bear patiently with an irksome relative, from whom one might hope to receive a large inheritance, but relinquish the virtue of patience when it comes to managing the everyday routines of a household. In the same way, the virtue of religion does not allow that one choose to observe the Lord's Day three times a month. In short, no Christian can decide to exercise a moral virtue only in a limited field of endeavor.

This sort of perfection throughout one's lifetime requires, to be sure, the divine initiative in our lives. "Blessed be the God and Father of our Lord Jesus Christ . . . who hath predestined us [in charity] unto the adoption of children through Jesus Christ unto himself" (Eph 1:3,[4],5). God's adopted sons and daughters, then, are joint-heirs with Christ (Rom 8:17), so they hold a certain claim to share in the inheritance of eternal life. There, *in patria,* the order of right reason attains a perfect identification with the order of charity. In other words, God will be all in all. In the meantime, the whole panoply of acquired and infused virtues ensures that not the smallest part of God's eternal plan, the *lex aeterna,* eludes fulfillment in our lives. So, Aquinas's teaching on the properties of the virtues draws out the full implications of another central New Testament teaching on the moral life: "For truly, I say to you, whoever gives you a cup of water to drink because you bear the name of Christ, will by no means lose his reward" (Mk 9:41). Or, as another doctor of the Church—St. Ambrose—explains it, "When we speak about virtue, we speak about Christ."[44]

CONCLUSION

Since it espouses a substantive doctrine of the good, the Christian tradition provides an intelligible foundation for the moral life and moral theology. Accordingly, the Christian can distinguish authentic human existence from its divers counterfeit forms. Even a young St. Augustine could testify that delight acts like a weight on the soul, "delectatio quasi pondus est animae"; therefore, he asserts, delight orders the soul, "delectatio ergo ordinat animam" (*De musica*, Bk. 6, chap. 11, no. 29). This observation, which finds its analogue in musical experience, suggests that delight signifies a soul well-ordered to its ends. More than anything else, the virtuous person delights in the practice of virtue. The saints recognize this delight as a sign of the perfection of charity. With this understanding, Church pastors, doctors, and theologians have explained virtue to their congregations and students throughout the Christian centuries.

The Aristotelian conception of "excellence of character" *ēthikē aretē* namely, that state of human perfection which belongs to the complete and well-formed human person, provided the philosophical point of departure for this study. However, as an essay in *theological* ethics, this book presents a systematic exposition of the moral virtues and Christian belief, sounding the various meanings and allusions in St. Paul's remark, "what matters is faith that expresses itself in love" (Gal 5:6). This opens up perspectives which lead us to regard specific spheres of the moral life as opportunities to advance in virtue. Other conceptions of the moral life, to be sure, remain viable options for theological ethics. But the present discussion argues for an intrinsic morality, one which could explain why a life of *recta ratio* and Gospel faith leads to virtue and delight. Such a starting-point in theological ethics differs significantly from where revisionist moral theories begin, namely, with an amalgam of compromise and debate about what constitutes the true good for men and women.

At the same time, the topic of moral virtue opens up a new field of inquiry for many students of theological ethics. Thus, this introduction to the theology of the moral virtues undertook to accomplish three major objectives: First, it presented virtue-centered morality as an integral part of Christian moral theology; second, it treated (as systematic theology requires) the basic elements which make up a theology of the moral virtues; and, third, it explained the actual relevance of the virtues and Christian faith by reference to those moral issues commonly disputed by contemporary theologians and ethicists.

While the general thrust of the exposition maintained a positive tone, references to other ways of talking about the virtues or to alternative models for theological ethics do appear throughout the course of the discussion. As these references clearly indicate, moral theology advances several major proposals for Christian living which give less prominence to the place of the moral virtues. For example, some theoreticians argue that the moral virtues, the gifts of the Holy Spirit, and the beatitudes describe well enough the inner dispositions of a Christian, but prove less helpful in solving the immediate problem of what one should do in a given moral situation. In other words, ethics must first of all concern itself with concrete choices. Since alternative systems often do in fact provide rational principles or guidelines for determining a course of action, it was necessary to insist that the moral virtues, directed by prudence, also equip an individual to make the proper decisions for a good life. Virtue educates us into a coherent way of thinking and judging. As the experience of so many Christian centuries demonstrates, virtuous *habitus* shape the individual so that he or she is capable of acting in a way which conforms to the norms of both right reason and evangelical truth.

Too many rational principles can actually thwart the work of moral theology. Casuistry, for example, so mimicked the conventions of jurisprudence that its workings left the conscientious Christian overly dependent on the opinions of experts. Thus, canon lawyers, not the moral theologian, served as the high priests of casuistry. But the case method of doing moral theology, prominent before the Second Vatican Council, succumbed under the weight of its own investigations. The theology of the moral virtues, on the contrary, makes the believer dependent chiefly on the grace of the Holy Spirit, who raises us to the dignity of children of God and makes our whole lives a filial and spiritual offering to God (cf. Rom 12:1).

Of course, this pneumatological side of the moral virtues urges the believer to embrace Christian instruction. Only exaggerated notions of autonomy—even those claimed by reason of conscience—require one to dispute legitimate authority in the Church. The virtuous life, on the other hand, seeks harmony with ecclesiastical moral teaching because it recognizes that the Magisterium faithfully and trustworthily represents the designs of the Eternal Law. By always doing the will of the heavenly Father, even unto death on a cross, Christ revealed the perfection of human virtue. Holiness of life, then, optimizes human freedom, it does not restrain it.

In short, the theology of the virtues persuades us to trust that God will remain faithful to his promise that everyone who believes in Jesus will find salvation, and that not one will be lost. Or, again as St. Ambrose reminds us, "When we speak about virtue, we speak about Christ." The Second Vatican Council expressed it this way: "Christ the Lord, the New Adam, in the very revelation of the mystery of the Father and of his love, fully reveals man to himself and brings to light his most high calling" (*Gaudium et spes,* no. 22). St. Paul learned on the road to Damascus that it is not easy to do battle with God. Rather, as the saints testify, we become truly free only when we enter into God's covenant.

Some contend that exact conformity to divine truth results in a moral homogeneity which ignores the variety of characteristics, temperaments, and traits which we encounter in members of the human species. But the virtues do not create automatons. Rather, the virtues and gifts of the Holy Spirit especially ensure that what is unique in each personality emerges with perfection. Although not everyone displays this perfection in the same way, the virtues nevertheless remain both connected and proportionally equal—to borrow Aquinas's image, "like the fingers on a hand"—in each believer. The unity and connection of the virtues likewise ensures that the Christian believer lacks nothing which is required for the right conduct of a human life. This accounts for the equilibrium which we see in the saints, no matter what strengths of character they may bring to Christian faith. Right reason provides the virtuous mean for the philosophers, but for the Christian, Christ himself is the prudent man.

Still, even the virtuous person can fall. The forgiveness of sins remains a specifically Christian teaching, one which allows the sinner to regain virtue in a way which the philosophers could not have imagined. The New Testament itself suggests that the need for forgiveness arises more often than some stiff moral theories like to consider. "'Lord, how often shall my brother sin against me, and I forgive him? As many as seven times?' Jesus said to Peter, 'I do not say to you seven times, but seventy times seven'" (Mt 18:21,22). St. Augustine speaks the truth about Christian forgiveness: it is Christ who forgets the sin, who encourages the repentance, and who crowns the perseverance. Of course, the saints do not endorse laxism with respect to keeping the commandments; rather, St. Augustine simply enunciates the dynamic of Christian growth and development which conforms exactly to the theology of the virtues.

Moral theology today has still to achieve the balance which Christian doctrine and life require. The controversies which have marked the post-conciliar period represent so many endeavors on the part of moral theologians to regain this balance. As happens in any attempt to retrieve values, conflicting points of view emerge. The present study, which represents one tradition of doing moral theology, takes its bearings from the Dogmatic Constitution on the Church, *Lumen gentium:*

> The followers of Christ called by God not in virtue of their works but by his design and grace and justified in the Lord Jesus have been made sons of God in the baptism of faith and partakers of the divine nature and so are truly sanctified. They must therefore hold on to and perfect in their lives that sanctification which they have received from God. (*Lumen gentium,* 40)

At the same time, since this theology of the moral virtues adopts the perspectives of St. Thomas Aquinas, especially on prudence and the moral conscience, it develops certain points which the conciliar documents leave more or less implicit. For example, virtue theory does not highlight the role of the Commandments and ecclesiastical precepts. Even so, one can appreciate why the Church continues to recommend that catechetical instruction include explicit reference to the Commandments. In fact, Aquinas also makes a point of showing how the moral virtues which develop around a given cardinal virtue relate to the precepts of the Decalogue. Moreover, the one who cultivates the moral virtues still holds to "the obedience of faith" (Rom 1:5), which demands fidelity to God's will and to the moral law. Still, moral instruction given according to the moral virtues, the gifts of the Holy Spirit, and the beatitudes ventures another course in theological ethics from that followed by pre-conciliar casuistry and other forms of moral legalism.

The saints teach us that in the eventide of life we shall be judged on our loves. As St. Augustine understood it, all the requirements of prudence, justice, fortitude, and temperance easily translate into love. The theology of the virtues aims directly at the Christian commandment that one love God above all things and the neighbor as oneself. Since our happiness depends on how we succeed in this task, we should suffer no compromise in matters of divine love. In the parable of the wise virgins, Christ urges us to watch carefully for we know not the day nor the hour. This state of evangelical preparedness, in brief, amounts to the practice of a virtuous life, that is, one ready to enter into the delight of the Lord.

NOTES

NOTES FOR INTRODUCTION

1. In his *De opificio Dei,* chap. 12, Lactantius (*c.* 240–*c.*320) adopted the etymology proposed by Cicero, namely that *virtus* derives from *vir.* But in the *Institutiones,* Bk 6, chap. 5, he gives the notion further precision by insisting that virtue is an interior reality which effectively shapes human capacities to accomplish good deeds. Hence, Lactantius, who used the latter work to commend revealed truth to the educated class, rejected the philosophical claim which identified virtue with knowledge. Rather, the author argues that the divine dignity (*dignatio divina*) established in those who accept the truth of the Gospel results in more than simply new information: "Verum scientia non potest esse virtus, quia non est intus in nobis, sed ad nos extrinsecus venit" (*PL* 6, col. 650).

2. For example, in *Enarrationes in Psalmos* 83, no. 11, Augustine identifies all virtue with the person of Christ himself: "Multae uirtutes, sed hic necessariae; et ab his uirtutibus imus in uirtutem. Quam uirtutem? Christum, Dei uirtutem, et Dei sapientiam. Ipse dat diuersas uirtutes in loco hoc, qui pro omnibus uirtutibus necessariis in conualle plorationis et utilibus dabit unam uirtutem, seipsum" (*Corpus Christianorum SL* 39, p. 1157). "Now we require many virtues, and from these virtues we advance to virtue itself. What virtue, you inquire? I reply: Christ, the very virtue and wisdom of God. He gives diverse virtues here below, and he will also supply the one virtue, namely himself, for all of the other virtues which are useful and necessary in this vale of tears."

3. *Enarrationes in Psalmos* 70, no. 10: "Quid est: tota die? Sine intermissione. In prosperis, quia consolaris; in aduersis,

quia corrigis; antequam essem, quia fecisti; cum essem, quia salutem dedisti; cum peccassem, quia ignouisti; cum conuersus essem, quia adiuuisti; cum perseuerassem, quia coronasti" (*Corpus Christianorum, SL* 39, p. 948).

4. For further information on the structure of casuistry, see Romanus Cessario, O. P., "Casuistry and Revisionism: Structural Similarities in Method and Content," in *"Humanae Vitae": 20 anni dopo,* Atti dell II Congresso Internazionale di Teologia Morale (Milano: Edizioni Ares, 1989), 385–409.

5. See Gregory E. Pence, "Recent Work on Virtues," *American Philosophical Quarterly* 21 (1984): 281-297, for a thorough account of the work done up to that date.

6. Precise interest in the theology of the moral virtues has begun to develop in European academic circles. For example, see the Tübingen dissertation of Eberhard Schockenhoff, *Bonum hominis. Die anthropologischen und theologischen Grundlagen der Tugendethik des Thomas von Aquin* (Mainz: Matthias-Grünewald-Verlag, 1987). Lee H. Yearley surveys the recent literature on virtue in "three separable but overlapping areas: philosophical inquiries, theological inquiries, and 'public philosophy'." The author gives the most attention, however, to the third category. See her "Recent Work on Virtue," *Religious Studies Review* 16 (1990): 1–9.

7. The Second Vatican Council's Declaration on Religious Liberty, *Dignitatis humanae,* no. 14.

8. The Second Vatican Council's Decree on Priestly Formation, *Optatam totius,* no. 16: "Special attention needs to be given to the development of moral theology. Its scientific exposition should be more thoroughly nourished by the scriptural teaching. It should show the nobility of the Christian vocation of the faithful, and their obligation to bring forth fruit in charity for the life of the world."

9. St. Thomas Aquinas (*c.* 1224–1274) occupies an important place among the shapers of Christian theology. For a discussion of the evolution of his moral theology, see Giuseppe Abbà, *Lex et virtus: Studi sull'evoluzione della dottrina morale di san Tommaso d'Aquino* (Rome: Libreria Ateneo Salesiano, 1983).

10. See Leonard Boyle, O.P., "The Setting of the *Summa theologiae* of Saint Thomas," Etienne Gilson Lecture Series 5 (Toronto: Pontifical Institute of Medieval Studies, 1982), p. 23. This

article provides valuable historical information on the originality of Aquinas's virtue theory.

11. Thus, in his *In Epistolam ad Galatas,* chap. 5, lect. 6, Aquinas explains: "Accipitur autem differentia donorum, beatitudinem, virtutum et fructuum ad invicem, hoc modo. In virtute enim est considerare habitum et actum. Habitus autem virtutis perficit ad bene agendum. Et si quidem perficiat ad bene operandum humano modo, dicitur virtus; si vero perficiat ad bene operandum supra modum humanum, dicitur donum. Unde Philosophus supra communes virtutes ponit virtutes quasdam heroicas: puta, cognoscere invisibilia Dei sub aenigmate est per modum humanum, et haec cognitio pertinet ad virtutem fidei, sed cognoscere ea perspicue et supra humanum modum, pertinet ad donum intellectus. Actus autem virtutis vel est perficiens, et sic est beatitudo, vel est delectans, et sic est fructus, et de istis fructibus dicitur Apoc., xxii, 2: *Ex utraquae parte lignum vitae afferens fructus duodecim."* "We can explain the difference between the gifts, the beatitudes, the virtues, and the fruits in the following way. First of all, virtue implies *habitus* and action. The *habitus* of virtue perfects good activity. And if the *habitus* perfects good activity according to a human mode, it is called a virtue. On the other hand, if it perfects good activity in a mode which surpasses the human, it is called a gift. So Aristotle, for example, considered certain heroic virtues apart from common virtues. We can apply this distinction as follows: to know the invisible things of God darkly, as in a mirror, remains a human kind of knowing, and such knowledge belongs to the virtue of faith; but to know these same things with heightened insight and beyond a human mode belongs to the gift of understanding. An act of virtue either perfects human conduct, in which case it produces a beatitude, or it causes delight, in which case it is called a fruit. The Book of Revelation 22:2 refers to these fruits: 'And from both parts of the tree of life hung twelve fruits.'"

12. *De moribus ecclesiae catholicae* Bk 1, chap. 15: "Quod si virtus ad beatam vitam nos ducit, nihil omnino esse virtutem affirmaverim, nisi summum amorem Dei" (*PL* 32, col. 1322).

NOTES FOR CHAPTER ONE

1. Amélie Rorty, ed., *Essays on Aristotle's Ethics* (Berkeley: University of California Press, 1980) collects a number of essays

which discuss specific aspects of Aristotle's ethical arguments. Arthur Flemming, "Reviewing the Virtues," *Ethics* 90 (1980): 587–595, provides a survey of the literature up to that date. For a recent example of moral philosophy's interest in Aristotle, see D. S. Hutchinson, *The Virtues of Aristotle* (London: Routledge and Kegan Paul, 1987). Finally, J. O. Urmson delivered the 1989 Aquinas Lecture at Blackfriars, Oxford entitled "Aristotle on Excellence of Character," *New Blackfriars* 71 (1990): 33–37.

2. P. T. Geach, *The Virtues* (Cambridge: Cambridge University Press, 1977). The chapters were originally delivered as the Stanton Lectures (1973–4). Although Geach's argument includes reference to theological issues, he nevertheless asserts: "I shall argue that the four traditional 'cardinal' virtues certainly are genuine virtues needed in human life. The need for the 'theological' virtues of faith, hope and charity depends on the truth of certain dogmas, which I shall not try to prove but only to expound" (p. v).

3. Ibid., p. viii.

4. Victor White, O. P., *Holy Teaching: The Idea of Theology According to St. Thomas Aquinas* (London: Aquin Press, 1958) provides a magisterial exposition of this important point. See also Thomas Gilby, O. P., *Christian Theology* (1a. 1), vol. 1 (New York: McGraw-Hill, 1964), pp. 58–87. [All references to the sixty-volume English translation of the *Summa theologiae,* under the general editorship of T. Gilby and T. C. O'Brien, will include author, title, and volume number. The part of the *Summa* and questions translated in the volume appear in parenthesis after the title. In quotations from this edition, the translations have been modified whenever clarity or consistency required.]

5. The interest in Protestant ethics is also limited, see Eilert Herms, "Virtue: A Neglected Concept in Protestant Ethics," *Scottish Journal of Theology* 35 (1982): 481–485.

6. Thomas Aquinas, *Summa theologiae* IIa–IIae, prologue. [References to the *Summa theologiae* follow the accepted practice, namely, the part of the work, e.g., Ia–IIae for the *prima secundae;* the question, e.g., q. 3; the article, e.g., a. 4; the specific part of an article if required, e.g., ad 2, for the reply to the second objection. References to the other works of Aquinas specify the title of the work along with the usual way of citing it.]

7. See Brian V. Johnstone, "The Meaning of Proportionate Reason in Contemporary Moral Theology," *Thomist* 49 (1985): 223–247, for a recent evaluation of the diverse meanings which authors give to the principle of proportionate reason.

8. Servais (Th.) Pinckaers, O. P., *Les sources de la morale chrétienne. Sa méthode, son contenu, son histoire* (Fribourg: Editions Universitaires, 1985), esp. pp. 244–326. See my discussion of this work in "Theology at Fribourg," *Thomist* 51 (1987): 339–362.

9. Ia–Iae, prologue.

10. Ibid.

11. Servais Pinckaers, O. P., treats this issue in *Ce qu'on ne peut jamais faire,* Etudes D'Ethique Chrétienne, no. 19 (Fribourg: Editions Universitaires Fribourg, 1986), esp. pp. 102–110, where the author replies to Richard McCormick's criticism that he commits an *ignoratio elenchi* by not addressing the fundamental distinction in theological ethics between good-bad and right-wrong. See *Theological Studies* 44 (1983): 76–80.

12. Ia–IIae q. 107, a. 1, ad 2.

13. *De peccatorum meritis et remissione* Bk. 2, chap. 5, no. 5: ". . . ita Deus, qui lux est hominis interioris, adjuvat nostrae mentis obtutum, ut non secundum nostram sed secundum ejus justitiam boni aliquid operemur" (*PL* 44, col. 153).

14. *Tractatus in I Johannem* Bk. 3, chap. 13: "Interior ergo magister est qui docet, Christus docet, inspiratio ipsius docet" (*PL* 35, col. 2004).

15. G. E. M. Anscombe, "Modern Moral Philosophy," in *Collected Philosophical Papers,* vol. 3: *Ethics, Religion and Politics* (Minneapolis: University of Minnesota Press, 1982), pp. 26–42.

16. See, for example, Douglas Den Uyl and Tibor R. Machan, "Recent Work on the Concept of Happiness," *American Philosophical Quarterly* 20 (1983): 115–134, for an example of the diversity of opinion held by philosophers on the question of human happiness.

17. The Second Vatican Council's Pastoral Constitution on the Church in the Modern World, *Gaudium et spes,* no. 24.

18. Leaving aside the abstract question of whether reason can discover every good required for personal well-being, there also exists the existential truth that all morality amounts to a *motus in Deum* lived in the fullness of love and worship. Thus, for

example, the satisfactory death of Christ establishes a unique form of worship which the acquired virtue of religion, in itself, could not ordain. Likewise, the humility and the obedience of Christ teach us the value of these virtues and others, such as penitence, in a way philosophers do not. L.-B. Gillon, O. P., "La hiéarchie axiologique des vertus morales selon saint Thomas," *Angelicum* 40 (1963): 3–24, elaborates this point. Although his discussion is not limited to changes effected by the grace of Christ, Basil Mitchell, *Morality: Religious and Secular* (Oxford: Clarendon Press, 1980), advances a convincing philosophical argument for the difference a religious ethics makes.

19. *Optatam totius,* no. 16: "Other theological disciplines should also be renewed by livelier contact with the mystery of Christ and the history of salvation. Special attention needs to be given to the development of moral theology. Its scientific exposition should be thoroughly nourished by scriptural teaching." Nonetheless, some authors did recognize virtue's place in fulfilling the Council's decree, for example, Jean-Marie Aubert, "Les vertus humaines dans l'enseignement scolastique," *Seminarium* 9 (1969): 417–433.

20. See Hutchinson, *Virtues of Aristotle,* esp. chap. 3, "Man: his ergon and his excellence."

21. Aquinas's teaching, e.g., in Ia-IIae q. 106, aa. 1, 2, that the whole of the New Law consists in the very grace of the Holy Spirit given to those who believe in Christ summarizes the earlier tradition on the power of grace. For example, consider St. Bernard's confidence expressed in his *Sermons on the Song of Songs* 61.3: "I may have sinned gravely. My conscience would be distressed, but it would not be in turmoil, for I would recall the wounds of the Lord: *he was wounded for our iniquities.* What sin is there so deadly that it cannot be pardoned by the death of Christ?"

22. Henry Sidgwick, "Clerical Engagements," *Pall Mall Gazette,* January 6, 1870, as cited in J. B. Schneewind, *Sidgwick's Ethics and Victorian Moral Philosophy* (Oxford: Clarendon Press, 1986), p. 40.

23. See Gerard W. Hughes, *God of Surprises* (Mahwah, N.J.: Paulist Press, 1985), pp. 40–54, for an example of this kind of biblical criticism.

24. See Aristotle, *L'Éthique à Nicomaque,* Tome 1, Première Partie, Introduction, ed. René Antoine Gauthier (Paris: Béatrice-Nauwelaerts, 1970), for a reliable history of how Christian thinkers put the *Nicomachean Ethics* to suitable use.

25. Aristotle, *Nicomachean Ethics,* trans. Terence Irwin, (Indianapolis: Hackett, 1985), Bk. 1, chap. 7 (1098a17,18). Subsequent citations follow this translation. For a more recent discussion of the same topic, see J. B. Schneewind, "Virtue, Narrative, and the Community," *Journal of Philosophy* 79 (1982): 653–663.

26. IIa–IIae q. 109, a. 3, ad 3.

27. See *Gaudium et spes,* no. 35: "Here then is the norm for human activity—to harmonize with the authentic interests of the human race, in accordance with God's will and design, and to enable men as individuals and as members of society to pursue and fulfill their total vocation."

28. M.-D. Chenu ably elaborates this point in his *Introduction to the Thought of St. Thomas Aquinas,* trans. A.-M. Landry, O. P., and D. Hughes, O. P. (Chicago: Henry Regnery, 1964), when he explains the absence of Christ in the *secunda pars:* "[T]he Incarnation is, however, in point of fact, a contingent event, and it enters in the *exitus-reditus* cycle only as an absolutely gratuitous work of God's absolutely free will" [p. 314]. Morals, on the other hand, which, like Christ, also form part of the human *reditus* to God, constitute a specifically determined plan whereby human behavior reaches its authentic goals. The necessity here remains hypothetical, i.e., given that God has freely chosen to create as he has. Thus, there exists a certain intelligibility and consistency in the natures which have been freely posited by God and which, therefore, one cannot simply set aside in moral theology.

29. See Richard A. McCormick, S. J., "Does Religious Faith Add to Ethical Perception?" in *Readings in Moral Theology,* No. 2: *The Distinctiveness of Christian Ethics,* ed. Charles E. Curran and Richard A. McCormick, S. J. (New York: Paulist Press, 1980), pp. 156–173. McCormick's own position on the matter also considers what he calls "a view of persons and their meaning" as another of Christian ethics' distinguishing features (p. 170).

30. Although Germain Grisez's numerous contributions to Christian ethics remain difficult to summarize, his massive *The Way of the Lord Jesus* vol. 1, *Christian Moral Principles* (New York: Franciscan Herald Press, 1983), esp. chaps. 26 and 27, suggests that the decision to follow one's personal vocation in imitation of Jesus Christ, especially in the context of the Church's sacraments, constitutes a distinctively Christian activity, but he does not consider the infused moral virtues as integral components of that vocation.

31. See Ia–IIae q. 61, a. 1: "Now human virtue, as we have said, is virtue as it corresponds to the perfect notion of virtue, which requires rectitude of appetite, for such virtue not only confers the faculty of doing well but also causes the performing of a good action." The reasons for this affirmation will appear in the subsequent discussion.

32. Geach, *Virtues*, p. vii.

33. Cf. *Physics* Bk. 3, chap. 1 (201a10,11). Aquinas remarks on this definition: "Hence, motion is neither the potency of that which exists in potency, nor the act of that which exists in act. Rather motion is the act of that which exists in potency, such that its ordination to its prior potency is designated by what is called 'act', and its ordination to further act is designated by what is called 'existing in potency'." See his *Commentary on Aristotle's Physics*, trans. R. J. Blackwell et al. (New Haven: Yale University Press, 1963), Bk. 3, Lecture 2, no. 285.

34. For example, Matthew Fox in "Is creation spirituality 'New Age'?" *Creation* 4, no. 3 (July/August 1988): 10,11, writes: "What might be called New Age movements in psychology, like Gestalt and Transpersonal psychology, were in some regard efforts to celebrate the 'Now' of the mystics and to celebrate our capacities for altered states of consciousness. These efforts to reawaken mystical and meditative traditions that honor the presence of the divine in all persons and at all times are laudable. These efforts at psychic healing and awakening are truer to mystical traditions than previous psychological schools of thought that, in fall/redemption fashion, were problem-oriented instead of power-oriented." Likewise, the use of the enneagram as a popular spiritual exercise promotes such syncretistic views. For example, see Maria Beesing, O.P., et al., *The Enneagram: A Journey of Self Discovery* (Denville, N.J.: Dimension Books, 1984).

35. See the Vatican Congregation for the Doctrine of the Faith, "Letter to the Bishops of the Catholic Church on Some Aspects of Christian Meditation" of December 14, 1989 for some important and balanced cautions concerning modish methods of spiritual renewal.

36. See Karl Rahner, *Foundations of Christian Faith*, trans. William V. Dych (New York: Seabury Press, 1978), p. 152. Of course, this volume provides only a convenient summary of Rahner's lengthier teaching as found, especially, in his *Theological Investigations*, 20 vols. (London: Darton, Longman & Todd, 1961–84).

37. For example, see the early post-war exchange between certain French Dominicans and their Jesuit counterparts in *Dialogue Théologique* (Saint-Maximum (Var.): Les Arcades, 1947).

38. John Mahoney, for instance, suggests that the Second Vatican Council adopted the "practical conclusions" of the 'anonymous Christian' hypothesis. See his *The Making of Moral Theology: A Study of the Roman Catholic Tradition* (Oxford: Clarendon Press, 1987), p. 100.

39. Rahner, *Foundations*, p. 430.

40. Ibid.

41. Charles E. Curran, *Directions in Fundamental Moral Theology* (Notre Dame, Ind.: University of Notre Dame Press, 1986), chap. 5, provides the main lines of criticism on natural law adopted by revisionist moral theologians.

42. Ia–IIae q. 109, a. 2.

43. Cf. *Quaestiones disputatae de veritate*, q. 25, a. 7, ad 5.

44. Henri Rondet, S.J., *The Grace of Christ: A Brief History of the Theology of Grace*, trans. and ed. Tad W. Guzie, S.J. (Westminster, Md.: Newman Press, 1966), still provides the best summary of the historical issues involved in this discussion. J.-H. Nicolas, O.P., *Les Profondeurs de la Grace* (Paris: Beauchesne, 1969), provides a magisterial discussion of the doctrinal issues involved in questions of human freedom and divine omnipotence from a Thomist perspective.

45. *Divinae Institutiones* Bk. 6, chap. 5: "Ergo sicut virtus non est bonum ac malum scire: ita virtus est bonum facere, malum non facere" (*PL* 6, col. 650).

46. Cf. *Nicomachean Ethics* Bk. 1, chap. 1 (1094a22–25).

47. In the *Republic* Bk. 4, chap. 6, Plato considers four chief or cardinal virtues: wisdom, courage or fortitude, temperance, and justice. Wisdom is the virtue of the rational part of the soul, courage of the spirited part, while temperance consists in the union of the spirited and appetitive parts under the rule of reason. Justice is a general virtue consisting in this, that every part of the soul performs its proper task in due harmony.

48. G. R. Evans, *The Thought of Gregory the Great* (New York: Cambridge University Press, 1986), studies this important teacher of morality for the Middle Ages. The Oxford Movement still provides the standard English translation of the *Moralia*. See *Morals on the Book of Job*, trans. John Henry Parker, 4 vols. (Oxford, 1844–50).

49. Stanley Hauerwas, *Character and the Christian Life: A Study in Theological Ethics* (San Antonio, Texas: Trinity University Press, 1975), esp. chap. 2, discusses the significant differences between Aquinas and Aristotle on this central issue for theological ethics.

50. Still, reluctance to recognize the distinction between the infused and acquired virtues usually leads to the displacement of virtues from a central place in moral theology. Thus, during the epoch of the casuists, for example, authors relegated the very discussion of virtue itself to treatises on spiritual or ascetical theology, as if the virtues constituted an exercise restricted to a moral elite.

51. See Odon Lottin, O.S.B., "Les vertus morales acquises sont-elles de vraies vertus? La réponse des théologiens de Pierre Abélard à S. Thomas d'Aquin," *Revue de théologie ancienne et médievale* 20 (1953): 13–39. For a more speculative discussion, see George P. Klubertanz, S.J., "Une théorie sur les vertus morales 'naturelles' et 'surnaturelles'," *Revue Thomiste* 59 (1959): 565–575.

52. *Lumen gentium*, no. 40.

NOTES FOR CHAPTER TWO

1. Nevertheless, theological literature on *habitus* remains scant. Some attempt to indicate their value to moral theology may be seen in an early apologetic work by Cardinal Satolli, *De*

habitibus. Doctrina S. Thomae Aquinatis in I–II, qq. 49–70 Summae Theologiae (Rome: Propagation of the Faith, 1897). In this century, see Placide de Roton, O.S.B., *Les Habitus. Leur caractere spirituel* (Paris: Labergerie, 1934) and George Klubertanz, *Habits and Virtues* (New York: Appleton-Century-Crofts, 1965). Some popular spiritual authors attempted to explain the importance of *habitus*, for example, Walter Farrell, O.P., and Dominic Hughes, O.P., *Swift Victory* (New York: Sheed and Ward, 1955). However, when Aquinas calls sanctifying grace an "entitative" *habitus* of the soul, he obviously suggests an analogical use of the concept. See Ia–IIae q. 50, a. 2.

2. Hauerwas, *Character and the Christian Life*, for example, signaled renewed interest in the use of Aristotelian concepts, especially *hexis*, among Protestant theologians. He argues "that Christian ethics is best understood as an ethics of character since the Christian moral life is fundamentally an orientation of self" (p. vii).

3. See *Nicomachean Ethics* Bk. 2, chap. 6 (1106b36); *Eudemian Ethics* Bk. 1, chap. 10 (1227b8). Hutchinson, *Virtues of Aristotle*, esp., chap. 6, provides a succinct exposition on Aristotle's teaching that virtue is a *hexis* of character. See also L. A. Kosman, "Being Properly Affected: Virtues and Feelings in Aristotle's Ethics," in *Essays on Aristotle's Ethics*, pp. 103–116.

4. St. Thomas develops his views on *habitus* in a small, well-crafted treatise in *prima-secundae*, qq. 49–54. Anthony Kenny, *Dispositions for Human Acts* (1a2ae.49–54), vol. 22 (New York: McGraw-Hill, 1964), chooses to translate the Latin term *habitus* as "disposition." Although he offers reasons for his choice (pp. xix–xxxiv), it seems preferable simply to accept the original Latin term *habitus* as serviceable for English usage.

5. For example, the scholastic adage, "*habitus medio modo se habet inter potentiam et actum purum.*" D. W. Hamlyn, "Behavior," *Philosophy* 28 (1953): 132–145, makes the same point. Movement, he writes, "arises out of a potentiality and may lead to a *hexis* (a state or disposition). The activity is the realization of that *hexis*. Perfect activity would be quite independent of any potentiality but human activities only approximate to this state of affairs which is characteristic of the divine" (p. 132). Aristotelian scholars generally share this view.

6. See G. E. M. Anscombe, "Thought and Action in Aristotle," in *Articles on Aristotle 2, Ethics and Politics*, ed. Jonathan Barnes et al. (New York: St. Martin's Press, 1977), pp. 61–71, for a discussion of some of the technical issues of interpretation involved in this statement.

7. See Ia–IIae q. 49, a. 3: "Utrum habitus importet ordinem ad actum." In the *sed contra*, Aquinas writes: "Augustine says that a *habitus* is 'something which permits action at need' [*De Bono Conjugali* chap. 21, 25; *PL* 40 390]. And Averroës says that a disposition is 'something which a man can exercise in action at will' (*Commentary on De Anima* Bk. 3, 18)." Bernard Ryosuke Inagaki also discusses this question in *The Philosophy of Habit* (Tokyo: Sobunsha, 1981), and in his article "Habitus and Natura in Aquinas," in *Studies in Medieval Philosophy*, ed. John F. Whippel (Washington: Catholic University of America Press, 1981), pp. 159–175: "The central thesis of my paper is that in his mature thought, Aquinas understood habitus in its essential relationship to human nature *qua* end. Another thesis, in support of the central one defended in this paper, is that according to Aquinas the cause of habitus is not acts or the repetition of acts, but some preexisting natural principle—in the final analysis, human nature itself" (p. 159).

8. Joseph Butler (1692–1752) developed his moral philosophy principally in response to the theories of Hobbes. See his *Fifteen Sermons* in *The Works of Joseph Butler*, ed. W. E. Gladstone, vol. 2 (Oxford: Clarendon Press, 1896), p. 63.

9. See the discussion in the *Nicomachean Ethics* Bk. 2, chap. 2 (1104a23–25), especially the importance Aristotle assigns to early character formation: "It is not unimportant, then, to acquire one sort of habit or another, right from our youth; rather, it is very important, indeed all-important."

10. See Servais Pinckaers's early article, "La vertu est tout autre chose qu'une habitude," *Nouvelle Revue Theologique* 80 (1960): 387–403.

11. However, see Jacques-M. Pohier, O.P., "Psychology and Virtue," *New Blackfriars* 50 (1969): 483–490.

12. For example, Vernon Bourke, "The Role of Habitus in the Thomistic Metaphysics of Potency and Act," in *Essays in Thomism*, ed. R. E. Brennan, O.P. (New York: Sheed and Ward, 1942), 103–109, offers a magisterial presentation on this subject.

In addition, Bourke's unpublished doctoral dissertation, "Habitus as a Perfectant of Potency in the Philosophy of St. Thomas Aquinas" (University of Toronto, 1938) provides the textual study which supports his conclusions.

13. Blaise Pascal (1623–1662), *Pensées*, ed. Brunschvicg, no. 294, makes this remark in the context of seventeenth-century debates between fanciful rationalists and glum Jansenists over the universality of natural law.

14. Cf. above, note 7. For a general study on Aquinas's use of philosophy in theology, see Per Erik Persson, *Sacra Doctrina: Reason and Revelation in Aquinas*, trans. Ross Mackenzie (Philadelphia: Fortress Press, 1970), esp. pp. 227ff.

15. See Pierre Benoit, O.P., for an original reflection on this doctrine in "Préexitence et Incarnation," *Revue Biblique* 77 (1970): 5–29.

16. The fourteenth-century Byzantine mystical writer, Nicholas Cabasilas (b. c. 1322) writes: "Continual union with Christ is necessary for souls if they wish to live fully and enjoy perfect rest. The eye cannot see without light: without Christ souls cannot have true life or peace." See his *Interpretation of the Divine Liturgy*, trans. Joan M. Hussey and P. A. McNulty, (1960), chap. 54. Unfortunately, the actual fragmentation of theology segregates moral theology from instruction about the dynamics of the participated divine life available to each believer through union with the Risen Christ.

17. See the excellent work by Benedict Ashley, O.P., *Theologies of the Body: Humanist and Christian* (Braintree, Mass.: Pope John Center, 1985) for a detailed study of this complex question. The author, moreover, emphasizes the contribution which the empirical sciences can make in theology.

18. Aquinas presents piety as the first of the social virtues which, along with religion, forms the constellation of virtues associated with the cardinal virtue of justice. Filial piety shapes a person's attitudes towards parents and native land. The pious son or daughter both respects parental instruction and fulfills the obligations which initiation into human society requires of its inexperienced members. As a virtue for beginners in life, filial piety demonstrates Aquinas's realist perspective on social mores and his conviction that social equality remains a goal to be achieved, rather than a starting-point of human experience. Filial

piety perdures in one's mature years, exercised by such activities as care for aged parents and patriotism. See IIa–IIae q. 101, aa. 1–4. See also E. Hugon, O.P., "La piété dans S. Thomas d'Aquin," *Vie Spirituelle* 15 (1927): 693–703.

19. Aquinas justified capital punishment on the grounds that the one guilty of certain heinous crimes, i.e., one who possessed chronically bad *habitus,* actually lost such a large measure of personal dignity that the moral theologian could no longer designate the object of the direct killing as human in an unqualified sense. Cf. IIa–IIae q. 64, a. 2, ad 3. See William E. May, "Aquinas and Janssens on the Moral Meaning of Human Acts," *Thomist* 48 (1984): 566–606.

20. See his extended treatment of this question in Ia–IIae, q. 49, a. 2, ad 3.

21. Bourke, "Role of Habitus," p. 106–107. "It is a metaphysical perfectant, heightening man's rational capacities to such an extent that he who acts with a habituated intellect and will, approaches the optimum performance of the strongest and most perfect human being." See also J. Chevalier, *L'habitude. Essai de métaphysique scientifique* (Paris: Boivin, 1929).

22. Aquinas stresses that the radical source or principal of human action, and consequently freedom, remains the human potencies/capacities, in Ia–IIae q. 49, a. 4: "But it is obvious that the nature and notion of a capacity is to be a source of action. And so every *habitus* whose possessor is a capacity is connected primarily with action." However, some later interpreters of Aquinas misconstrued the role that *habitus* plays in the formation of human activity. For example, the Spanish commentator Francisco de Suarez, S.J. (1548–1617) in his *Disputationes Metaphysicae,* disp. 44, sect. 1, no. 6, defined *habitus* as a "qualitas quaedam permanens et stabilis de se in subjecto, per se primo ordinata ad operationem, non tribuens primam facultatem operandi, sed adjuvans et facilitans illam." For Suarez, in other words, while *habitus* help and facilitate human behavior, the *habitus* themselves remain extrinsic to the actual capacity for action. One school of Thomist theological interpretation followed Suarez on this point, thereupon encouraging the portrayal of *habitus* as if it were a commodity one would acquire to make a machine run better. For further information, see Leon Mahieu, *Francois Suarez. Sa Philosophie et les rapports qu'elle a avec sa*

théologie (Paris: Desclée, De Brouwer & Cie, 1921), pp. 325–340.

23. The renaissance commentator Thomas de Vio Cajetan, O.P. (1469–1534) expresses it this way: "Disponitur enim, omne quod disponitur, ad actum aliquem; nec opus est disponi quod unius tantum est capax; et dispositio habentis est partes, i.e. partialia : ex ratione enim varietatis secundum bene vel male, diversitas habetur modorum." See his *Commentarium in Iam–IIae*, q. 49, a. 4, which may be found in the Leonine edition, vols. 4–12 (Rome 1888–1906) of the *Summa theologiae*.

24. See Ia-IIae q. 49, a. 4.

NOTES FOR CHAPTER THREE

1. See Boniface Ramsey, *Beginning to Read the Fathers* (New York: Paulist Press, 1985), esp. chap. 4 "The Human Condition," for a brief, but pellucid discussion of this complex topic in patristic writings.

2. See St. Augustine's *De Trinitate* Bk. 15, chap. 7, no. 10 and chap. 8, no. 11, for some typical examples of what he teaches on this matter. For a good study of how an Eastern Father treats the same topic, see W. J. Burghardt, *The Image of God in Man according to Cyril of Alexandria*, Studies in Christian Antiquity 14 (Washington, D.C.: Catholic University of America Press, 1957).

3. Some ethicists critcize this approach to teleology. They feel it is impossible to condense the practical goods of an ethical life into a single good-to-be-sought. On the other hand, Anthony Kenny argues that Aristotle remains guiltless of the fallacy attributed to him by Peter Geach and others, namely, that there is something that is the last term of every series whose successive terms stand in the relation 'chosen for the sake of.' Rather, says Kenny, happiness for Aristotle is at least one supreme end. Kenny, nonetheless, does accuse Aquinas of being entrapped by Geach's purported Aristotelian fallacy. See his "Aristotle on Happiness," in *Articles on Aristotle 2, Ethics & Politics*, p. 26. However, Jean Porter, "Desire for God: Ground of the Moral Life in Aquinas," *Theological Studies* 47 (1986): 48–68 explains the distinctively theological aspect of Aquinas's assertion that there

does exist a final term to human striving. But in her *The Recovery of Virtue: The Relevance of Aquinas for Christian Ethics* (Louisville: Westminster/John Knox, 1990), Porter wonders whether Aquinas's teleological frame of reference allows for performing actions "without reference to any wider aim" (p. 76). In the course of her discussion, however, she fails to take full account of Aquinas's view that divine beatitude serves as formal specifying cause of each action in the moral life. In this sort of debate, Thomas Gilby's comment is apposite, namely, that end so dominates the *secunda pars* that it should be read to say what it means.

4. See Ia–IIae q. 3, a. 8. In order to distinguish the pronounced difference between Aquinas and Aristotle on this point, see W. F. R. Hardie, "Aristotle on the Best Life for a Man," *Philosophy* 54 (1979): 35–50.

5. John Farrelly, O.S.B., *Predestination, Grace, and Free Will* (Westminster, Md.: Newman Press, 1964), gives a good account of the classical doctrine on predestination and its relationship to the moral life.

6. At the very start of his treatise on the virtues, Aquinas writes that "the virtue of anything has to be judged in reference to a good. Human virtue, therefore, which is an operative *habitus*, is a good *habitus* and productive of good" (Ia–IIae q. 55, a. 3).

7. See Ia–IIae q. 54, a. 3 where Aquinas develops this view within the larger context of his moral theology.

8. One contemporary author who grasps the practical significance of this classical feature of virtue theory is Yves R. Simon, *The Definition of Moral Virtue*, ed. Vukan Kuic (New York: Fordham University Press, 1986), esp. chaps. 2–4.

9. See Burghardt, *Image of God*, p. 4.

10. See Ia–IIae q. 54, a. 3. For Aquinas, the measure of the moral good and bad depends upon the harmonization of activity with right reason. Vice results from following some other measure than that which right reason ordains. But divine grace causes *habitus* in the Christian which render the believer capable of works which are "divinizing."

11. The mention of divine virtue suggests a field of inquiry which evades mere philosophical or, for that matter, psychologi-

cal investigation. The theologian alone can expound on the infused or divine virtues.

12. Although MacIntyre does not develop a specifically theological argument, he does point out that the early monastic communities provided the chance for a shared vision of what constitutes Christian existence. See his *After Virtue* (Notre Dame, Ind.: University of Notre Dame Press, 1981), especially chap. 18. Contemporary theology also sees the connection between the Church and the virtuous life: "The holiness of the Church is always manifest and must show itself by the fruits of grace which the Spirit produces in the faithful" (*Lumen gentium*, 39).

13. See Ambrosiaster (an unknown fourth-century author of commentaries on thirteen Pauline epistles), *Commentary on I Corinthians*, chap. 8: "Dum enim charitatem, quae mater omnium bonorum est . . . " (*PL* 17, col. 226). Most medieval writers ascribed this work to St. Ambrose.

14. Theories on the superfluity of the acquired moral virtues find their origin in the medieval theologians. Yet, later spiritual authors, such as St. Francis DeSales (1567–1622), following John Duns Scotus (1265–1308) on this point, also chose to speak about the moral virtues only in the context of charity.

15. This theme frequently appears in authors who appropriate Rahner, without much nuance, on the thorough-going penetration of the created order by divine grace. For example, Timothy O'Connell, *Principles for a Catholic Morality* (New York: Seabury Press, 1978) commenting on Colossians 1:15–17, writes: "This is a description of cosmic Christology, of the relationship of Christ and creation. And in essence it proclaims that we may be human. It is permitted to be human, Christ himself permits it. . . . Be human! No more and no less! Christ permits it, and Christ demands it. That is the central conviction of the Christian faith. And it is the fundamental premise of the following principles of Christian ethics" (p. 41). This unambiguous determination as regards the complex theological issues which surround the debates on nature and grace means that, for this author, "Christian" virtues emerge only in the pursuit of an authentic human existence.

16. See Romans 7:13–25 for St. Paul's classic description of the inner Christian struggle.

17. For a reliable survey of the general question, see Jean-Marie Aubert, 'Debats autour de la morale fondamentale,' *Studia Moralia* 20 (1982): 195–222. For the particular case of truth-telling, see the interesting research of Boniface Ramsey, "Two Traditions on Lying and Deception in the Ancient Church," *Thomist* 49 (1985): 504–533.

18. For example, Garth Hallett observes: "In traditional precept ethics, the reasoning employed on behalf of various norms often smuggled in moral values before their time. . . . The telling of falsehoods was labelled 'lying', the taking of property was labelled 'stealing', the killing of innocents was labelled 'murder', and so forth . . . " (p. 129). See his "The Place of Moral Values in Christian Moral Reasoning," *Heythrop Journal* 30 (1989): 129–149. Hallett, who advances a proportionalist argument, wants to put an embargo on what he considers "moral values smuggled in," so he continues: "Granted, no ends, however desirable, can justify *morally* evil means; but they can and often do justify nonmoral ('physical', 'ontic', 'premoral') evils" (p. 130). The author directs our attention to his *Reason and Right* (Notre Dame, Ind.: University of Notre Dame Press, 1984), esp. pp. 85–94, for fuller analysis and numerous examples of this kind of moral reasoning.

19. See Oscar Brown, *Natural Rectitude and Natural Law in Aquinas* (Toronto: Pontifical Institute of Medieval Studies, 1981), esp. pp. 1–12, for an exceptionally well-done analysis of the function which Aquinas assigns to the Eternal Law in theological ethics.

20. See the very good work of Joseph Incandela, "Aquinas's Lost Legacy: God's Practical Knowledge and Situated Human Freedom," doctoral dissertation, Princeton University, 1986.

21. Thus, Timothy O'Connell, *Principles*, chap. 14, "The Nature of Natural Law," gives one example of how little contemporary theologians grasp the authentic place which natural law holds in Christian moral theology. One could suppose that the author had mistakenly read G. W. Leibniz (1646–1716) on harmony in the universe, instead of Aquinas on natural law.

22. William E. May, "The Natural Law and Objective Morality: A Thomistic Perspective," in *Principles of Catholic Moral Life*, ed. William E. May (Chicago: Franciscan Herald Press, 1981), pp. 151–190, provides much needed clarification of this

controverted point. Also, see Martin Rhonheimer, *Natur als Grundlage der Moral: Die personale Struktur des Naturgesetzes bei Thomas von Aquin: Eine Auseinandersetzung mit autonomer und teleologischer Ethik* (Innsbruck: Tyrolia, 1987), for a contemporary philosophical perspective on this central topic for ethics.

23. See the standard work by Chenu, *Introduction*, pp. 129–136, for a discussion of this central feature of theological methodology in the Middle Ages.

24. See *Petri Pictaviensis Sententiarum libri quinque* Bk. 3, chap. 1 (*PL* 211, col. 1041). Peter of Poitiers, who taught theology in Paris from 1167 until his death in 1205, stands among those authors who generally withstood the accommodation of theological science to philosophy occasioned by the twelfth-century introduction of Aristotle into the West. Accordingly, he identified virtue with grace and stressed the divine agency in virtue formation by adding the phrase, "without us," to the definition already found in the *Sentences* of "Master" Peter Lomard (c. 1100–60). Nevertheless, as O. Lottin has pointed out, we owe the definition to the Lombard, who modified an actual text of St. Augustine by adding a fundamentally Augustinian thesis on the gratuity of grace. Thus, *Petri Lombardi libri IV Sententiarum* Bk. 2, dist. 27, chap. 5, defines virtue as "bona qualitas mentis, qua recte vivitur, et qua nullus male utitur, quam Deus solus in homine operatur" (ed. Quaracchi, 1916, p. 446, n. 1). For more information, see O. Lottin, "Les premières définitions et classifications des vertus au moyen age," *Revue des Sciences Philosophique et Theologique* 18 (1929): 369–389.

25. Ia-IIae q. 55, a. 4.

26. See, for example, Aristotle's account of decision in *Nicomachean Ethics* Bk. 3, chap. 3 (1113a10–17) where he talks about virtue as technique for action, "about what promotes the end."

27. Commenting on Galatians 2:20, Aquinas writes: "The oldness of sin is removed by the cross of Christ, and the newness of spiritual life is conferred. Therefore the Apostle says, 'with Christ I am nailed to the cross,' i.e., concupiscence or the inclination to sin, and all such have been put to death in me through the cross of Christ. . . . Thus, therefore, does Christ beget a new life in us, after the oldness of sin has been destroyed." See his

Commentary of St. Paul's Epistle to the Galatians chap. 2, lect. 6, trans. F. R. Larcher, O.P. (Albany: Magi Books, 1966), p. 62.

28. See Ceslaus Spicq, O.P., *Vie morale et Trinité Sainte selon Saint Paul* (Paris: Editions du Cerf, 1957), esp. chap. 2, "L'initiative divine."

29. The calling of the Christian entails progressively to "conform himself to the image of the Son" (Rom 8:21). Also C. E. O'Neill, O.P., *The One Mediator* (3a. 16–26), vol. 50 (New York: McGraw-Hill, 1965), esp. chap. 6, "Adoptive Sonship," explains the substance of Aquinas's teaching in IIIa q. 23.

30. Cyril of Jerusalem (c. 315–86) speaks directly to this point: "Though you be a publican or fornicator, yet hope for salvation. 'The publicans and harlots are entering the kingdom of God before you.' Paul testifies to this when he says: 'Neither fornicators nor idolaters,' nor the rest, 'will possess the kingdom of God. And such were some of you, but you have been washed, and you have been sanctified.' He did not say, some of you 'are,' but some of you 'were.'" See his *Third Catechesis*, no. 8 (*PG* 33, col. 439).

31. Suarez, for example, adopted the Scotistic position and so described virtue simply as a predicamental relation, not a quality of being. Thus, virtue approaches the status of positive law in the casuists' systems, namely, an extrinsic standard by which actions are measured. See Mahieu, *Suarez*, pp. 359ff. However, Aquinas stresses another point of view when he affirms that virtue is an operative *habitus*. See Ia-IIae q. 55, a. 2, ad 1.

32. For further information on the position of Scotus, see P. Raymond, "Duns Scot," *Dictionnaire de théologie catholique*, vol. 4.2, cols. 1904–1909.

33. Aquinas emphasizes this relationship of virtue to personal character. "It should be observed, however," he wrote, "that as modifications of substance and non-subsistant forms are called beings, not because they themselves have existence as things, but because a thing is affected by them, so also things are called good or one because thereby a thing is good or one, and not by a oneness or goodness distinct from the thing. Thus also virtue is called good because by it something is good" (Ia-IIae q. 55, a. 4, ad 1).

34. See his remarks in *De moribus ecclesiae catholicae* Bk. 1, chap. 6: "Nemo autem dubitaverit quin virtus animam faciat optimum" (*PL* 32, col. 1314).

35. See *Nicomachean Ethics* Bk. 2, chap. 6. (1106a15). St. Thomas cites this text in the *sed contra* of Ia-IIae q. 55, a. 3, according to the version of *Aristotelis Latinus*: "virtus est quae bonum facit habentem, et opus eius bonum reddit," that is, "virtue is what makes its possessor good and his works good likewise."

36. See how Peter Geach develops this point in *The Virtues*, chap. 1, "Why men need the virtues?"

37. Philippa Foot discusses the whole question of why philosophers are willing to see, for example, true courage and temperance even when a bad person does an evil work. See her essay, "Virtues and Vices" in *Virtues and Vices and Other Essays in Moral Philosophy* (Berkeley: University of California Press, 1978), p. 15.

38. This amounts to urging theologians, according to their own methods, towards a task similar to that which G. E. M. Anscombe challenged philosophers to do in her article, "Modern Moral Philosophy," namely, to elaborate an adequate statement concerning the essential goods which perfect human nature.

39. See Pinckaers, *Les sources*, pp. 134–143.

40. "Activity, like existence," insists Aquinas, "belongs to the composed whole; it is what exists that acts. A compound, however, has its substantial being through its substantial form, while it acts by virtue of a power dependent on its substantial form. Thus an accidental form by which a substance acts, such as the heat of something hot, is related to it much the same way the soul's power is related to the soul" (Ia q. 77, a. 1, ad 3). This doctrine forms part of Aquinas's general anthropology as set forth in the *prima pars*.

41. See Ia-IIae q. 56, a. 1.

42. Ia-IIae q. 56, a. 2.

43. But also see Hans Kung, *Eternal Life? Life after Death as a Medical, Philosophical, and Theological Problem*, trans. Edward Quinn (Garden City, N.J.: Doubleday, 1984).

44. Philip Keane, *Sexual Morality: A Catholic Perspective* (New York: Paulist Press, 1977), p. 38. The author claims that

the following authors use the fundamental option approach to sin: Charles E. Curran, John W. Glaser, Bernard Häring, Richard A. McCormick, and Timothy E. O'Connell.

45. See Aquinas's treatment on the dual function of charity in the moral life, i.e., as the "form" of the other virtues but also with its own proper objects in IIa–IIae q. 23 and qq. 25–27 respectively.

46. We find many discussions of this point in various journals of popular psychology. For a more scientific approach, see N. J. H. Dent, *The Moral Psychology of the Virtues* (Cambridge: Cambridge University Press, 1984). Mortimer J. Adler, *Ten Philosophical Mistakes* (New York: Macmillan Publishing Company, 1985), esp. chap. 2, "The Intellect and the Senses," notes that diverse views on the relationship of the human mind to the senses forms the basis for different opinions on how emotion can affect behavior. In short, those who follow the empiricist position that the human mind is a single cognitive power, however complex, differ from those who, following the position of classical philosophy, accept the division of the human mind into two quite distinct cognitive powers: sense and everything to which sense gives rise, and intellect, able to understand, judge, and reason.

47. The Franciscan doctor St. Bonaventure (*c.* 1217–1274), in particular, could not bring himself to accept that divine grace could sustain such a direct contact with materiality. Although he understood why philosophers might put fortitude and temperance in the sense appetites, the dignity of the infused virtues, he argued, would not permit theologians to do the same. See *Commentaria in IV Libros Sententiarum* (Quaracchi edition, 1887) Bk. III, dist. 33, a. 1, q. 3, "Utrum virtutes cardinales sint in parte animae rationali, an in ea parte, quae solum obtemperat rationi."

48. Adherents of value-free psychology especially reject what appears to them as a form of religiously sanctioned repression. Mitchell, *Morality: Religious & Secular*, esp. pp. 30–46, explains how "romantic humanism" reacts as well against false constraints.

49. See Ia–IIae q. 56, a. 4.

50. Aquinas actually quotes the *Politics* Bk. 1, chap. 2 (1254b5) in the text of Ia–IIae q. 56, a. 4, ad 3.

51. Ia–IIae q. 56, a. 4, ad 3.

52. See W. D. Hughes, "Virtue in Passion," in *Virtue* (1a2ae. 55–67), vol. 23 (New York: McGraw-Hill, 1969), pp. 245, 246. For further information on how the scholastics understood human emotion, see Mark D. Jordan, "Aquinas's Construction of a Moral Account of the Passions," *Freiburger Zeitschrift für Philosophie und Theologie* 33 (1986): 72–97.

53. This teaching finds a reflection in the orthodox eucharistic teaching on transubstantiation. St. Augustine, for example, taught that the moral lives of those who share in the eucharistic sacrifice exhibit the same kind of acceptable transformation as the elements of bread and wine themselves. See his *City of God* Bk. 10, chap. 6.

54. Later he will specify this principle: "Because to draw particular conclusions from universal principles is not the work of simple intelligence but of reasoning, the irascible and concupiscible are said to obey the reason rather than the intellect" (Ia q. 81, a. 3).

55. See Ia q. 82, a. 4, ad 1.

56. The citation is from the Song of Solomon 5:2. St. Ambrose makes this point in his *Expositio psalmi CXVIII*, sermo 12, no. 14: "considera quando maxime pulsat januam tuam deus uerbum: cum repletum est caput eius rore nocturno. in tribulatione etenim et temptationibus positos uisitare dignatur, ne quis forte succumbat uictus aerumnis. repletur ergo caput eius rore uel guttis, quando corpus eius laborat nos" (*Corpus Scriptorum EL* vol. 62, pp. 258, 259).

57. "Beatus ergo ille cuius pulsat ianuam Christus. ianua nostra est fides quae totam domum, si fuerit robusta, communit" (ibid).

NOTES FOR CHAPTER FOUR

1. Colman O'Neill, O.P., "The Fullness of Christ's Sacrifice," *Word and Spirit* 5 (1984): 44–60, develops this point in the context of biblical and systematic theology.

2. See Hebrews 9:11–10:18, which spells out the characteristics of Christ's sacrifice, esp. 9:12, 25–26, which insists that the offering was *made once for all*.

3. For a discussion of some movements which fostered this view of the Christian life, see Ronald A. Knox, *Enthusiasm* (Westminster, Md.: Christian Classics, 1983), pp. 176–230.

4. Jean-Joseph Surin, S.J. (1600–65), *Lettres spirituelles*, ed. Cavallera, t. II, p. 120, cited in Leszek Kolakowski, *Chrétiens sans Eglise. La Conscience religieuse et le lien confessionnel au XVIIe siècle*, trans. Anna Posner (Paris: Editions Gallimard, 1969), p. 467. This exhaustive study of seventeenth-century French spirituality provides a more balanced example of Cartesian spirituality in the figure of Pierre de Bérulle (1575–1629), esp. pp. 405–413.

5. See his *Sermo* 169, chap. 11, no. 13: "Ergo fecit nescientem, justificat volentem. Qui ergo fecit te sine te, non te justificat sine te" (*PL* 38, col. 923).

6. See his *Commentaria in Joannem*, chap. 26, no. 2: "Quem trahat et quem non trahat, quae illum trahat et illum non trahat, noli velle judicare, si non vis errare. Semel accipe, et intellege nondum traheris? ora ut traharis" (*PL* 35, col. 1607).

7. The archetype for all such controversies remains the patristic conflict between St. Augustine and Pelagius. Although more recent studies are available, J. Tixeront, *History of Dogmas*, translated from the fifth French edition (Westminster, Md.: Christian Classics, 1984), pp. 432–505, provides the basic elements of the debate.

8. See Aquinas's account of how Old Law moral precepts contained all of the virtues in Ia-IIae q. 100, a. 2.

9. The celebrated controversies *De auxiliis* at the end of the sixteenth century examined the various ways in which divine grace can be said to cooperate with human freedom. At present, the mood and interests in theology result, unfortunately, in leaving the question largely to philosophers of religion. But see M. Corvez, O.P., "Motion divine et grace actuelle," *Revue Thomiste* 49 (1949): 225–241.

10. Ia-IIae q. 109, a. 9, ad 2. In the treatise on the New Law of grace (qq. 109–114), Aquinas mentions the Holy Spirit twenty-seven times; four of these references include the formula "the grace of the Holy Spirit."

11. Aquinas makes this point when he ascribes to Christ the perfection of each of the moral virtues: "Since grace was at its very best in Christ, it gave rise to virtues which perfected each

of the faculties of the soul and all its activities. In this way Christ had all the virtues" (IIIa q. 7, a. 2). Although Aquinas principally aims to describe the sacred humanity of Christ, his overall theological design includes establishing the person of Christ as the font and center of the whole moral life.

12. See his *Eighteenth Catechesis*, no. 23 (*PG* 33, col. 1043).

13. Charles Curran insists that "from a more philosophical-anthropological perspective the relationality-responsibility model fits in better with the emphasis on historicity." Hence Curran argues for what he calls a more adequate conscience theory. See *Directions in Fundamental Moral Theology* (Notre Dame, Ind.: University of Notre Dame Press, 1986), pp. 230ff.

14. Brian V. Johnstone examines the way moral theologians discuss practical reason in "The Structures of Practical Reason: Traditional Theories and Contemporary Challenges," *Thomist* 50 (1986): 417–446. J. O. Urmson, "Aristotle's Doctrine of the Mean," *American Philosophical Quarterly* 10 (1973): 223–230, critiques the intellectualist bias which sees emotion's role in virtue as either peripheral or beguiling. All in all, contemporary discussions of practical reason mostly reflect the parameters established by Kantian and other forms of purely rationalist moral philosophy. On the other hand, since *recta ratio* depends on the Eternal Law, the scholastic notion of right reason transcends the impartial character of Kantian ethics with respect to the appetites.

15. Ceslaus Spicq, O.P., *Charity and Liberty in the New Testament*, trans. F. V. Manning (New York: Alba House, 1965) provides one of the few essays on the subject of freedom in the New Testament which takes knowledge of moral truth seriously into consideration. See also his more recent work, *Connaissance et Morale dans la Bible* (Fribourg: Editions universitaires, 1985), which points out the general importance of cognition in the New Testament's account of morality.

16. Urmson, "Excellence of Character," p. 35.

17. *Nicomachean Ethics* Bk 2, chap. 6 (1106a16,17).

18. See *Gaudium et spes*, no. 48: "Husband and wife, by the covenant of marriage, are no longer two, but one flesh. By their intimate union of persons and of actions they give mutual help and service to each other, experience the meaning of their unity, and gain an ever deeper understanding of it day by day. This

intimate union in the mutual self-giving of two persons, as well as the good of the children, demands full fidelity from both, and an indissoluble unity between them."

19. See his *De moribus ecclesiae catholicae* Bk. 1, chap. 15: "prudentia, amor ea quibus adjuvatur ab eis quibus impeditur, sagaciter seligens" (*PL* 32, col. 1322).

20. IIa-IIae q. 47, a. 1, ad 1.

21. Ia-IIae q. 107, a. 4.

22. For a classic analysis of this important point, see R. Garrigou-Lagrange, O.P., "La prudence. Sa place dans l'organisme des vertus," *Revue théologique* 9 (1926): 411–426. But for a more contemporary study, see Charles O'Neill, "Is Prudence Love?" *Monist* 58 (1974): 119–139.

23. For an accurate appraisal of the status of contemporary research on this point, see Stephen D. Dumont, "The Necessary Connection of Moral Virtue to Prudence According to John Duns Scotus—Revisited," *Recherches de Théologie ancienne et médiévale* 55 (1988): 184–206.

24. Although, as Dumont's study indicates, we do not possess a critical edition of *In Libros Sententiarum*, Bk. 3, d. 36, a. 2, the actual textual evidence supports the view that Duns Scotus denied that prudence necessarily requires moral virtue. For further information, see Allan Wolter, *Duns Scotus on the Will and Morality* (Washington, D.C.: Catholic University of America Press, 1986). In addition, the position of Scotus certainly prejudiced subsequent German Nominalism, so that the influential Gabriel Biel, for example, adopted much of the Scotistic view on prudence. See John L. Farthing, *Thomas Aquinas and Gabriel Biel: Interpretations of St. Thomas Aquinas in German Nominalism on the Eve of the Reformation* (Durham, N.C.: Duke University Press, 1988), esp. chap. 5, "Ethics."

25. Thus, Richard M Gula, S.S., mistakenly identifies the following situation as "a prudential judgment" concerning artificial contraception: "A Catholic married couple, who give presumptive authority to the church's teaching on marriage and want to live by it, know that for now they can best preserve their marriage and family life by using artificial means of birth control. Given their limited moral capacity, and the limiting factors of their marital and familial situation, they are unable to live by what the church prescribes in its official teaching for marriage.

Their choice to use artificial contraception is a prudential judgment. It should not be confused with dissent." See his *Reason Informed By Faith: Foundations of Catholic Morality* (New York: Paulist Press, 1989), p. 160.

26. Alasdair MacIntyre, *A Short History of Ethics* (New York: Macmillan, 1966), provides a readable survey of these various schools of rational ethics.

27. For example, see his *De virtutibus in communi*, a. 8.

28. See Yves R. Simon, "Introduction to the Study of Practical Wisdom," *New Scholasticism* 35 (1961): 1–40, for a full presentation of these pivotal points in realist morals. Also, Michel Labourdette, "Conscience practique et savoir moral," *Revue Thomiste* 48 (1948): 142–179.

29. Aquinas discusses this definition taken from Boethius's *De duabus naturis* (*PL* 64, col. 1343) in Ia q. 29, a. 1. For an excellent treatment of how the Thomist tradition accounted for the uniqueness of the created person, see T. U. Mullaney, "Created Personality: The Unity of Thomistic Tradition," *New Scholasticism* 29 (1955): 369–402.

30. See Ia-IIae q. 91, a. 2.

31. Lucien Richard, O.M.I., provides a recent survey of opinion on the question of a specifically Christian morality in *Is There a Christian Ethics?* (New York: Paulist Press, 1988).

32. Aquinas probes the question of the relationship of positive morality to the law of nature in Ia-IIae q. 100, a. 1, where he inquires whether all the moral precepts of the Old Law come under the law of nature. There he distinguishes between natural law precepts, precepts perceived only by the morally wise, and precepts which require divine instruction.

33. Ia-IIae q. 94, a. 1.

34. Ia-IIae q. 94, a. 2, ad 2. Also see Ia-IIae q. 94, a. 1, where Aquinas describes *synderesis* as "habitus continens praecepta legis naturalis, quae sunt prima principia operum humanorum." Timothy C. Potts, *Conscience in Medieval Philosophy* (Cambridge: Cambridge University Press, 1980), pp. 45–60, gives a good historical study of Aquinas's use of *synderesis*. For a complete discussion of its role according to an authoritative Thomist point of view, see Labourdette, "Connaisance practique et savoir moral," esp. pp. 149ff.

35. At present there exists considerable discussion, even among Thomists, concerning the place basic goods hold in theories of natural law. Russell Hittinger provides a useful summary of the different schools of thought in his *A Critique of the New Natural Law Theory* (Notre Dame, Ind.: University of Notre Dame Press, 1987), especially chaps. 1–2.

36. Aquinas in IIa-IIae q. 49, treats eight component parts of prudence: memory, insight, teachableness, acumen, reasoned judgment, foresight, circumspection, and caution.

37. The scholastics used the term *res* in a broad and analogical sense. For instance, since he proceeds from the mutual love of the Father and Son, they even called the Holy Spirit the *res amoris*, that is, the "Thing of Love." But as *res* points chiefly to the complete constitution of any physical or moral entity, theological ethics uses the term to refer to the particular, concrete goals or ends of the different virtues. These ends, in turn, illustrate a moral order which accords with how divine Providence ordains that creatures, including the free actions of men and women, should reach their perfection.

38. See *The Degrees of Knowledge*, translated from the 4th French edition under the supervision of Gerald B. Phelan, (New York: Charles Scribner's Sons, 1959), p. 463.

39. See Ia-IIae q. 57, a. 4. The attention of specialists should be drawn to the treatise of Cajetan on this material, especially *In Iam-IIae* q. 57, a. 5.

40. Ralph McInerny offers a brief but lucid description of this point in *Ethica Thomistica: The Moral Philosophy of Thomas Aquinas* (Washington, D.C.: Catholic University of America Press, 1982), p. 38ff.

41. See Leo Scheffczyk, "Christology in the Context of Experience: On the Interpretation of Christ by E. Schillebeeckx," *Thomist* 48 (1984): 383–408, for some pertinent observations on the subject. Similarly, one can consult the works of Baron von Hügel (1852–1924) on the question of experience in Christian theology.

42. See William van der Marck, "Ethics as a Key to Aquinas's Theology: The Significance of Specification by Object," *Thomist* 40 (1976): 535–554.

43. Admittedly certain later scholastics overworked the term with the result that human persons became conflated with infra-

personal objects. However, to state that a person can be a moral object for another person simply affirms that the person-as-object stands in some kind of interpersonal relationship to the other. See the excellent treatment of this matter by T. C. O'Brien, *Faith* (2a2ae. 1–7), vol. 31 (New York: McGraw-Hill, 1966), esp., "Objects and Virtues." Also L. Dewan, "'Objectum': Notes on the Invention of a Word," *Archives d'Histoire Doctrinale et Litteraire du Moyen Age* 48 (1981): 37–96, esp. pp. 64–78, 91, 93–94.

44. See John Finnis, *Natural Law and Natural Rights* (Oxford: University Press, 1980), especially chap. 4, for an exposition of the various ways thinkers have enumerated lists of basic or fundamental goods.

45. The literal translation runs: "how I am according to my appetites, in such a way I view the end of human existence."

46. *Inferno*, Canto V, 37–39: "Intesi ch'a cosi fatto tormento enno dannati i peccator carnali, che la ragion sommettono al talento."

47. Ia-IIae q. 17, a. 1.

48. *Inferno*, Canto III, 16–18: "Noi siam venuti al loco ov'io t'ho detto che tu vedrai le genti dolorose c'hanno perdutto il ben dell'intelletto."

49. Ia-IIae 59, a. 4, ad 1.

50. The psychological bases for this truth involve the way in which the intellect and will include each other in their operations. See, for example, Ia q. 82, a. 4 ad 1.

51. Aquinas makes this point clearly in *De virtutibus in communi*, a. 12, ad 12.

52. The distinction reflects Aristotle's classification of the virtues of character in *Nicomachean Ethics*, Bk. 2, chap. 7.

NOTES FOR CHAPTER FIVE

1. Ia-IIae q. 62, a. 1. ad 2. See also, W. J. Hill, O. P., *The Three-Personed God* (Washington, D.C.: Catholic University Press, 1982), esp. pp. 273–286, for a discussion of the proper relations of the indwelling persons in the souls of the just.

2. The indefatigable researcher Dom Odon Lottin provides us with the details of this doctrine's development in his standard

work on medieval moral theology, *Psychologie et morale aux XIIe et XIIIe siècles* (Paris: Gembloux, 1949), especially Part III, I.

3. Ia-IIae q. 63, a. 4, ad 2.

4. I am indebted to Alasdair MacIntyre, *After Virtue,* esp. chap. 4, "The Predecessor Culture and the Enlightenment Project of Justifying Morality," pp. 44–47, for the anecdote concerning the French encyclopedist Denis Diderot (1713–1784).

5. Ia-IIae q. 85, a. 3.

6. In the short treatise, written in French, which summarized his vast philosophical output, Leibniz wrote: "L'ame suit ses propres loix, et le corps aussi les siennes, et ils se rencontrent en vertu de l'harmonie préétablie entre toutes les substances, puis'quelles sont toutes des representations d'un même Univers." See *Die Philosophischen Schriften von Gottfried Wilhelm Leibniz,* ed. C. J. Gerhardt (Berlin: Weidmannsche Buchhandlung, 1885), p. 620.

7. See the fine study of Aquinas's view of original sin by T. C. O'Brien in *Original Sin* (Ia2ae, 81–85), vol. 26 (New York: McGraw-Hill Book Company, 1964), esp. Appendix 9, pp. 154–161.

8. Jacques Maritain, *Person and the Common Good,* trans. John J. Fitzgerald (Notre Dame, Ind.: University of Notre Dame Press, 1972), outlines the importance this metaphysical distinction holds for the practical affairs of ethics and politics.

9. See Ia-IIae q. 63, a. 1.

10. Ibid.

11. See *Nicomachean Ethics* Bk. 2, chap. 1 (1103b3–7).

12. Simon, *Definition of Moral Virtue,* p. 51.

13. See Ia-IIae q. 63, a. 2.

14. Oscar Brown observes: "Thus, in the (Christian) religious perspective of Aquinas, the order or direction to be pursued (*regula, lex*) is first and foremost one created for, not by, man. That *ordo* is precisely the eternal law, God's law (*lex divina*). The sinner seeks to remake that order, even if only with reference to himself, and to make the law, therefore, by and for himself." See his *Natural Rectitude and Divine Law,* p. 11.

15. See his *Rhetoric* Bk. 1, chap. 9 (1366a36,37).

16. See IIa-IIae q. 123, a. 8. Aristotle makes a similar observation in *Nicomachean Ethics* Bk. 3, chap. 9 (1117b8–16).

17. See the discussion of this point in Ia-IIae q. 53, aa. 1–3. Also *De virtutibus in communi,* a. 11.

18. See Ia-IIae q. 63, a. 2, ad 2.

19. Ibid. See also *De virtutibus in communi,* a. 9, ad 5.

20. Odon Lottin makes this point in *Principes de Morale,* Tome II. *Compléments de doctrine et d'histoire* (Louvain: Editions de L'abbaye du Mont César, 1946), p. 215. See also the texts collected in his "Les vertus cardinales et leurs ramifications chez les théologians de 1230 à 1250," *Psychologie et Morale aux XIIe et XIIIe siècles,* Bk. 3, no. 12.

21. *Quaestiones in III librum Sententiarum* d. 36, no. 28.

22. The Dominican Durandus of Saint-Pourçain, a nominalist theologian, along with three secular masters, Henry of Ghent, Godfrey of Fontaine, and Thomas de Bailly, held similar views on the theology of the infused virtues. Henry and Godfrey, moreover, were probably students of Aquinas at Paris.

23. For further discussion, see A. De Sutter, O.C.D., "De virtutum moralium infusarum existentia controversia recentior," *Ephemerides Carmeliticae* 14 (1963): 413–431.

24. St. Francis DeSales also held this opinion on the sufficiency of charity and faith to account for the supernatural life. See John Harvey, "The Nature of the Infused Moral Virtues," *Catholic Theological Society of America Proceedings* 10 (1955): 172–217.

25. Ia-IIae q. 63, a. 3. This text comes from *Treatise on the Virtues,* trans. Vernon Bourke (Notre Dame, Ind.: University of Notre Dame Press, 1966). Cajetan wrote that the infused virtues may be distinguished from the acquired on three counts: first, cause; second, formal object; third, relation to the end. See his *In Iam-IIae* q. 63, a. 3, no. 2.

26. IIa-IIae q. 17, a. 2. Aquinas continues to explain: "That is simply to say that we should hope for nothing less from God than his very self; his goodness, by which he confers good upon creaturely things, is nothing less than his own being."

27. See Thomas Gilby, O. P., *Purpose and Happiness* (1a2ae. 1–5), vol. 16 (New York: McGraw-Hill, 1968), p. 153. For further discussion of this issue, see appendix 5, "The Vision of God," pp. 153–155. The Thomistic commentorial tradition offers different solutions for solving the puzzle of a natural desire that can only find perfect completion in a supernatural End. One

approach, which seems to make as much sense as any in a matter that, in the final analysis, involves the free workings of divine grace, runs as follows: The natural desire for God in the human creature constitutes a desire of the will, an elicited appetite, as it is called, for a good somehow perceived. Yet the desire remains impotent of itself—in this sense, that it presupposes no active natural power proportionate to the object. The creature, however, does possess an openness, what theologians call an "obediential potency," to the action of a supernatural cause on this potency. The desire, moreover, remains conditional, one that can be frustrated when a condition, namely God's free act of will, is not given. Thus the object of the desire remains wholly supernatural, but the desire itself remains natural on the part of the subject for it rises from our knowledge of created things; remains free, since it can be withheld or committed otherwise than to the thought of seeing God; and is an authentic expression of a mind and will open to the whole of reality without reserve.

28. See *Gaudium et spes,* no. 18.

29. Ia-IIae q. 3, a. 8. A. Gardeil, *La structure de l'âme et l'experience mystique* I (Paris: Gabalda, 1927), pp. 271–307, offers an extended commentary on this topic.

30. *Gaudium et spes,* no. 18, also states: "God has called man, and still calls him, to be united in his whole being in perpetual communion with himself in the immortality of the divine life."

31. The scholastics termed this the *finis operantis,* which they also distinguished from the *finis operis,* viz., the property which delineates a particular action to be a complete moral reality. Usage, however, varies among different authors. See Michel Labourdette, O. P., "La morale chrétienne et ses sources," *Revue Thomiste* 77 (1977): 625–642. In general, the distinction between the *finis operantis* and the *finis operis* remains misunderstood by contemporary theologians. Some, for example, suppose that the *finis operis* provides nothing morally determinative, unless one also clearly establishes the specifics of the *finis operantis.* Such theologians would argue that without taking account of the intent of the masturbator, self-abuse, even though a specifically defined action, still remains altogether morally undetermined. But moral realists insist that, once correctly established, the *finis operis* actually embodies moral meaning in a given action. Thus,

the results of anesthesia on a patient differs from ordinary drunk-enness in a college student according to the *finis operis,* despite what amount to identical physical symptoms, and not simply on account of the diverse intentions for altering consciousness. See Augustus Mansion, "L'Eudémonisme aristotélicien et la morale thomiste," *Xenia Thomistici,* 1st edition (Rome, 1925), pp. 429–449, for discussion of this point in reference to teleological ethics.

32. See W. D. Hughes, *Virtue* (1a2ae. 55–67), vol. 23 (New York: McGraw-Hill, 1968), pp. 247–248, for a brief treatment of this issue.

33. See John 9:1–41. Sight, unlike an infused virtue, remains a radically natural capacity.

34. See IIa-IIae q. 134, a. 2. Aquinas describes magnificence as a special virtue if it is understood in the strict meaning of the term, namely, the realization of some great work.

35. On the other hand, Cardinal Ratzinger emphasizes the distinctive quality of New Testament morality when he writes: "It is impossible to distill out what is specifically Christian by excluding everything that has come about through contact with other milieux. Christianity's originality consists rather in the new total form into which human searching and striving have been forged under the guidance of faith in the God of Abraham, the God of Jesus Christ." See his *Principles of Christian Morality* (San Francisco: Ignatius Press, 1986), p. 53. A theology of the infused virtues seeks to account for "the new total form" which Christian faith gives to the moral life.

36. *In III Sententiarum* d. 33, q. 1, a. 4.

37. Ibid., a. 2, quaestiuncula 4.

38. See the treatment in D. M. Prümmer, O. P., *Manuale Theologiae Moralis secundum Principia S. Thomas Aquinatis,* I (Freiburg-im-B.: Herder & Co., 1923), pp. 310–313, for an ex-ample of how the requirements of simplification for the sake of seminary education resulted in a somewhat distorted "standard" version of theology.

39. See the work of Y.-M. Congar, O. P., "Le traité de la force dans la *Somme théologique* de S. Thomas d'Aquin," *Angelicum* 51 (1974): 331–348.

40. *In III Sententiarum* d. 33, q. 1, a. 2, quaestiuncula 4, ad 2.

41. Of course, "separation from family" needs some explaining, even (or perhaps precisely) as an element of New Testament morality. For some, it is actual physical separation, but for others it is not. The absolute requirement for all is that God come first and family ties not take precedence over one's obligations to God. How this is expressed will differ for different people, depending on state in life and personal vocation.

42. Heinz Schürmann suggests some of these points in "How Normative Are the Values and Precepts of the New Testament? A Sketch," esp. 1, "Jesus' Deeds and Words as the Ultimate Ethical Norm," in *Principles of Christian Morality*, pp. 18–26.

43. Even so, when the noted Dominican manualist Dominic Prümmer wrote that "the rule of infused temperance is the *lex divina* which prescribes" such and such, he perhaps unwittingly led people to think that *lex divina* simply meant a divinely revealed precept. This, of course, would trim considerably the meaning that Aquinas intends by the term "*formaliter.*"

44. IIIa q. 7, a. 2.

45. See IIIa q. 15, a. 2; q. 18, a. 2.

46. IIIa q. 7, a. 2, ad 3.

47. *Quaestio disputata de virtutibus cardinalibus*, a. 4, ad 2.

48. See the "personalist" explication of this principle, the *sequela Christi*, in Fritz Tillmann, *Handbuch der katholische Sittenlehre* III, *Die Idee der Nachfolge Christi* (Dusseldorf: Druck und Verlag L. Schwann, 1934), esp., pp. 44–79.

49. For further information on the virtue of justice itself, see D. Mongillo, O. P., "La struttura del 'De justitia,' *Summa theologiae* II-II qq. 57–122," *Angelicum* 48 (1971): 355–377.

50. *De virtutibus in communi*, a. 9. Aquinas affirms that the infused cardinal virtues remain with the believer in glory. Of course, they no longer produce actions required for reaching the ultimate End, rather they facilitate actions "which befit one already resting in the End." See his *De virtutibus cardinalibus*, a. 4; also Ia-IIae q. 67, a. 1.

51. R. Snackenberg, *The Moral Teaching of the New Testament* (New York: Herder & Herder, 1971), pp. 168–196, discusses this fundamental characteristic of New Testament morality.

52. *Quaestio disputata de virtutibus cardinalibus*, a. 4.

53. Ia-IIae q. 110, a. 2.

54. C. E. O'Neill, *Sacramental Realism: A General Theory of the Sacraments* (Wilmington, Del.: Michael Glazier, 1983), provides a fuller account of the theology of baptism, esp. chap. 5.

55. See *Catechismus ex decreto Concilii Tridentini ad parochos, Pii V jussu editus,* ed. and pub. Paulum Minutium (Romae, 1566), Part II, *De Sacro Baptismo,* chap. 2, q. 39. For historical background on this important document in the history of theological ethics, see Guy Bedouelle, O. P., "The Birth of the Catechism," *Communio* 10 (1983): 35–52.

56. See his discussion in IIa-IIae q. 154, a. 2.

57. *In IV Sententiarum* d. 14, q. 2, a. 2.

58. *Letter to Barnabas* 11:11 (PG 2, 760).

59. Lucien Cerfaux, *Le chrétien dans la théologie paulinienne* (Paris: Les Editions du Cerf, 1962), elaborates on this important theme for New Testament theology.

60. See *De potentia* q. 3, a. 15, ad 14: "The ultimate end is not the communication of goodness, but rather divine goodness itself. It is from his love of this goodness that God wills it to be communicated. In fact, when he acts because of his goodness, it is not as if he were pursuing something that he does not have, but, as it were, willing to communicate what he has. For he does not act from desire of the end, but from love of the end."

61. For example, see St. Paul's own personal testimony in 2 Corinthians 13:8.

62. *De virtutibus in communi,* a. 10, ad 14.

63. Ibid., ad 15.

64. "Quam laetus illic Christus fuit, quam libens in talibus seruis suis et pugnauit et uicit protector fidei et dans credentibus tantum quantum se credit capere qui summit." *Epistulae* X, chap. 3 (*Corpus Scriptorum Ecclesiasticorum Latinorum,* vol. III, pars. II, p. 492).

65. We ordinarily treat this question in connection with the theological virtues. Moreover, even authors from within the Thomistic tradition explain this matter differently. For a discussion of a related topic, see Antoninus Finili, O. P., "On the Virtue of Religion and the Infused Moral Virtues," *Dominican Studies* 3 (1950): 78–88.

66. See *De virtutibus in communi* a. 10, ad 4.

67. See *Quaestiones disputatae de Veritate* q. 29, a. 7, for Aquinas's discussion of this christological thesis.

68. *On Repentance,* Bk 1, chap. 8: "Cur baptizatis, si per hominem peccata dimitti non licet? In baptismo utique remissio peccatorum omnium est, quid interest utrum per poenitentiam, an per lavacrum hoc jus sibi datum sacerdotes vindicent? Unum in utroque mysterium est" (*PL* 16, col. 497). This observation of St. Ambrose occurs in the context of countering a certain sacramental rigidity promoted by the Novatian heresy. In addition, see Cyril of Jerusalem, *Second Catechesis,* "On Repentance and the Remission of Sin" (*PG* 33, cols. 379–424), for another instance of how the Fathers understood the relation between baptism and penitence.

69. See Kolakowski, *Chrétiens sans Eglise,* especially chap. 8, "La mystique condamnée. Le quiétisme," pp. 492–566, for an astute interpretation of the writings and personalities of figures such as Miguel Molinos and Madame Guyon.

70. For example, see St. Irenaeus, *Adversus haereses* III, chap. 18 (*PG* 7, 932).

NOTES FOR CHAPTER SIX

1. For example, Peter Geach comments on the second characteristic, what he calls the unity of the virtues, as follows: "Corrupt habits of action in any area destroy the habit of prudence; but without prudence as a regulator no behavioral habit is genuinely virtuous; so loss or lack of any one behavioral virtue is fatal both to prudence and to all other behavioral virtues." Still, he takes exception to the thesis because, as he puts it, "human inconsistency" might allow someone to exercise unsound practical judgment in one area, but not in another. See his *Virtues,* p. xxxi. Geach's objection, however, considers the acquired virtues from a philosopher's point of view.

2. See Servais Pinckaers, O. P., "La morale chrétienne et ses sources: Ecriture, tradition et magistére," *Anthropotes* 3 (1987): 25–42, where the author emphasizes the need to read St. Paul without imposing artificial categories of interpretation, especially those which derive from non-biblical sources.

3. Promoted especially by Jesuit theologians, Molinism strongly emphasizes the role of human agency and initiative in the moral life. This school of thought, named after the Spanish Jesuit Luis de Molina (1535–1600), places human freedom on something of an equal footing with divine grace, "like two men rowing a boat." Dominicans argued that Molinism compromised the absolute priority of the divine initiative in the life of the infused virtues, but the Church declined to issue an authoritative ruling on the matter.

4. The text of Dominic Bañez (1528–1604) is found in his commentary on the *Summa theologiae, In IIam-IIae* q. 23, a. 4 (1586 edition, col. 540). Also see Aquinas's remarks in Ia-IIae q. 64, a. 3, ad 2.

5. *Moralia* Bk 22, chap. 1: "Una virtus sine aliis aut omnino nulla est aut imperfecta" (*Corpus Christianorum SL* vol. 143a, p. 1093).

6. *Letter to Eustochium, virgin,* no. 108, no. 20: "Difficile est modum tenere in omnibus. . . . Quod nos una et brevi sententiola exprimere possumus 'Ne quid nimis' " (*PL* 22, col. 898).

7. See his *Commentarius in Canticum Canticorum,* 9: "Propterea quod virtus est media inter duo vitia, nempe inter defectum honesti et exsuperationem" (*PG* 44, col. 971).

8. *Nicomachean Ethics* Bk. 2, chap. 6 (1106b37–1107a3).

9. See her *Story of a Soul,* trans. John Clarke, O. C. D. (Washington: ICS Publications, 1976). For example, Thérèse wrote, "Yes, I feel it, when I am charitable, it is Jesus alone who is acting in me, and the more united I am to him, the more also do I love my Sisters."

10. Although the theological virtues do not render practical reasoning superfluous, it is significant that the term *synderesis* does not appear, for example, in Aquinas's *Commentary on Romans,* where theological faith predominates. Pierre Leroy, "La conscience dans le *Commentaire ad Romanos* de S. Thomas," 2 vols. (Ph.D. dissertation: Université Catholique de Louvain, 1970), pp. 50, 235. See also D. J. Billy, C.Ss.R., "Grace and the Natural Law in the *Super Epistolam ad Romanos Lectura:* A Study of Thomas' *Commentary on Romans* 2:14–16," *Studia Moralia* 26 (1988): 15–37.

11. Vernon J. Bourke, *History of Ethics,* vol. 1, *Graeco-Roman to Early Modern Ethics* (New York: Doubleday, 1970),

esp. chaps. 8 and 9, provides a survey of the ethical features of both British Egoism and Continental Rationalism.

12. Fr. Richard McCormick offers a series of concrete examples of this method: "For example, a lie consists in telling what is false without commensurate reason and therefore directly or formally causes the error of another. Theft is the taking of the property of another without commensurate reason. Mutilation is surgery without a commensurate reason. Murder is killing without commensurate reason. Contraception is intervention into the fertility of the conjugal act without commensurate reason." See his *How Brave a New World?: Dilemmas in Bioethics* (New York: Doubleday, 1981), p. 417. For the background to this position, see Louis Janssens, "Ontic Evil and Moral Evil," *Louvain Studies* 4 (1972): 115–156; reprinted in *Readings in Moral Theology, No. 1, Norm and the Catholic Tradition,* ed. Charles E. Curran and Richard A. McCormick, S. J. (New York: Paulist Press, 1979), pp. 40–93.

13. See Pope John Paul II, *Reconciliatio et poentitentia,* no. 16: "In speaking of situations of sin or denouncing certain situations and attitudes as socially sinful . . . the Church knows and teaches that these cases of social sin are the fruit, the accumulation and the concentration of numerous personal sins."

14. *Commentary on the Nicomachean Ethics,* Bk. 5, lect. 10.

15. John Oesterle, *Treatise on the Virtues,* p. 135, n. 25.

16. See IIa-IIae q. 154, a. 11. See also the reply to the third objection where Aquinas emphasizes that the quest for sexual pleasure as an end in itself accounts for the moral evil of unchaste activity.

17. Aquinas, for whom the importance of an issue may be roughly estimated by the amount of space he devotes to its discussion, treats all of the so-called sins "against nature" in a single article dealing with certain vices against chastity, *viz.,* IIa-IIae 154, a. 11. Certain philosophers recognize that some forms of sexual behavior do not serve to advance human dignity, see, for example, Roger Scruton, *Sexual Desire: A Moral Philosophy of the Erotic* (New York: Free Press, 1986).

18. Ia-IIae q. 64, a. 3, ad. 2.

19. R. Bernard, O. P., *La Vertu,* vol. 2 (1a-2ae. 61–70) in *Editions de la Revue des Jeunes* (Paris: Desclée, 1934), p. 330.

20. Ia-IIae q. 106, a. 3.

21. See John P. Langan, S. J., "Augustine on the Unity and the Interconnection of the Virtues," *Harvard Theological Review* 72 (1979): 81–95.

22. *Letter to Jerome,* no. 167, chap. 2. (*PL* 33, col. 735).

23. See n. 1 above.

24. Sometimes confusion, e.g., of humility with wimpishness, or courage with aggressiveness, contributes to the impression that these virtues remain irreconcilable.

25. See Lottin, *Principes de Morale,* pp. 196, 197: "Le chancelier Philippe cependant établit une distinction entre charité spéciale et charité générale; la charité spéciale nous fait aimer Dieu pour lui-même, la charité générale nous fait aimer pour Dieu tout ce qui conduit à Dieu, et par exemple les actes de toutes les autres vertus théologales et morales." In addition, chapter 13 of the same book provides a survey of opinions held by various authors on this topic.

26. For example, see *Nicomachean Ethics* Bk. 6, chap. 13.

27. See Ia-IIae q. 65, a. 1.

28. *Moralia* Bk. 22, chap. 1.

29. Aquinas gives Aristotle the credit for pointing out the connection of the virtues based on what Aquinas calls their "matter." See Ia-IIae q. 65, a. 1.

30. Ibid., ad. 1. See also Cajetan's commentary on this reply.

31. Aquinas proposed two different standards to measure virtue: extension and intensity. Extension refers to the breadth or scope of the virtue's control, *viz.,* what kind of goods the virtue promotes or evils it restrains; according to extension, then, "a virtue's being greater or less is based on the things which it encompasses" (Ia-IIae q. 66, a. 1). Intensity, on the other hand, refers to the grasp a particular individual has on virtue. Of course, one distinguishes *habitus* from a disposition on the basis that the former is firmly rooted in the one who possesses it, but this does not exclude that even a fully formed virtue can be more or less established in different people.

32. Ia-IIae q. 65, a. 1. Peter Lumbreras, O. P., "Notes on the Connection of the Virtues," *Thomist* 11 (1948): 218–240, provides a good summary of the classic commentators' views on this thesis: "Perfecta autem virtus moralis est habitus inclinans in bonum opus bene agendum" [perfect moral virtue is a *habitus* which disposes one to act well in a good work].

33. In Cajetan's terse phrase: "Virtus moralis eligit medium in propria materia: simpliciter, i.e., secundum se et ut in eam redundant aliae materiae. Ergo exigit rectam rationem sui secundum se et secundum comparationem ad alias" [Moral virtue chooses its mean in its own matter in two ways: simply, that is in its own area of interest, and in order that the other virtues might flow back into it. So moral virtue requires right reason for itself both in its own area of interest and by comparison with the other virtues] (*In Iam-Iae* q. 65, a. 1. no. 8).

34. *In IIam-IIae* q. 23, a. 7. no. 1. Cajetan argues that the difference between the way theologians and philosophers consider virtue arises from the existence of a human destiny which transcends that which we discover in creation. Philosophers call certain virtues perfect without qualification because they are not obliged to take this destiny—beatitude—into account, but theologians recognize these same virtues as perfect only as far as the genus of virtue goes. Because theologians must figure beatitude into their analysis, they call these virtues imperfect in themselves.

35. See J.-M. Aubert, "La spécificité de la morale chrétienne selon saint Thomas," *Le Supplément* 92 (1970): 55–73, for a discussion of this issue.

36. IIa-IIae q. 23, a. 8, ad. 3. Although "charging them with life" remains a free translation of "imperando ipsos," the sense of the phrase does reflect the substance of Aquinas's view on how form imperates acts, for example, "Charity is said to be the form of the other virtues, not as exemplar or essential, but rather as efficient, inasmuch as it impresses its form on all of them" (Ibid., ad 1).

37. See Ia-IIae q. 65, a. 2. Also see Jacques Maritain, *La loi naturelle ou loi non écrite,* ed. Georges Brazzola (Fribourg: Éditions Universitaire, 1986), for an optimistic view about the universality of natural law ethics despite the objections of social anthropologists.

38. Ia-IIae q. 109, a. 8. In general, the whole of this question considers the need for divine grace. Cornelius Ernest, *The Gospel of Grace* (1a2ae. 98–105), vol. 30 (New York: McGraw-Hill, 1972), pp. 98, 99, comments on this particular article: "Human freedom is such that it needs to be liberated by being established in a communion with God; only then can it achieve security from recurrent lapse into sin. Until it is so established it can still

choose rightly and avoid sin in any given case, but not in every case; it can only govern the whole course of a human life when it has found itself in submission to God."

39. See John 15:1–11. In fact, the Johannine writings as a whole continually emphasize that the believer must remain personally united with Christ in order to do the works that please God.

40. *De Trinitate* Bk. 6, chap. 4: "Si enim uirtutes quae sunt in animo humano, quamuis alio atque alio modo singulae intellegantur, nullo modo tamen separantur ab inuicem, ut qui cumque fuerint aequales uerbi gratia in fortitudine, aequales sint et prudentia et justitia et temperantia" (*Corpus Christianorum SL 50*, p. 233).

41. For Aquinas, this position represents his mature reflection on the matter, as Cajetan observes: "Ita non dicam virtutes aequales secundum habitum et non secundum actum [an earlier position of Aquinas in *In III Sententiarum*, d. 36] sed dicam quod virtutes secundum formale in habitu sunt aequales; secundum vero materiale sunt inaequales: quod est dicere: habitus virtutum ut perficiunt subjecta ut mota a prudentia vel caritate sunt aequales proportionaliter, ut vero perficiunt eadem ut tendentia in proprias materias sunt inaequales" [I do not contend that the virtues are equal according to *habitus* but not according to act. Rather, I affirm that the virtues are equal in form as *habitus*, but are unequal in their material element. In other terms, the *habitus* of the virtues as they perfect a subject who is moved by prudence or charity are equal proportionally. Yet they remain unequal insofar as they perfect the same subject with respect to his or her (simple) inclination towards the virtue's specific area of interest] (*In Iam-IIae* q. 66, a. 2. no. 2).

42. Ia-IIae q. 66, a. 2.

43. See Pinckaers, *Sources,* pp. 150–173, for a discussion of the importance which St. Augustine attaches to the Sermon on the Mount for the moral life. Aquinas also incorporates each of the biblical beatitudes (Mt 5:3–10) into his treatment of the virtues and the gifts of the Holy Spirit.

44. *Explanatio psalmi XXXVI*, no. 65: "loquamur ergo dominum Jesum, quia ipse est sapientia, ipse est uerbum et uerbum dei . . . cum de uirtute loquimur, ipse [Christus] est" (*Corpus Scriptorum EL,* vol. 64, pp. 123–124).

INDEX OF SUBJECTS

INDEX OF NAMES

INDEX OF SCRIPTURE
REFERENCES